ORAL LITERATURE OF THE ASIANS IN EAST AFRICA

Oral Literature
of the Asians
in East Africa

Mubina Hassanali Kirmani
Sanaullah Kirmani

EAST AFRICAN EDUCATIONAL PUBLISHERS
Nairobi • Kampala • Dar es Salaam

CONTENTS

*Dedicated to
all children and to their children's children
so that they know their heritage
and learn to appreciate each other*

FOREWORD

Reading this manuscript put me in touch with my cultural history and made me realise how much literary abundance I had forgotten, or was not even aware of. Memories came flooding in from my childhood days of the stories I had heard, the proverbs and riddles that had enthralled me and the games that we used to play. It was an enriching experience that I should never have 'grown out of'.

Oral literature is not frozen as in the printed word; it allows for self-expression, renewal, innovation and creativity. It gives us an understanding of our roots and ourselves; in short our culture. Our thinking, our lifestyles, our values and our whole philosophy of life is based on that culture – a culture that has been transmitted for generations through the spoken word.

Culture is dynamic, it takes on new forms and manifestations as we seek to adapt to changing circumstances and whether it is through bedtime stories in an urban setting or at *cucu*'s (grandmother's) feet under a tree in a village; the all-important function of oral literature continues to shape our society.

And it is not just the individual who benefits from having a vibrant and meaningful cultural base, our nation does too. A country's oral literature reflects its social, economic and political institutions; it is an expression of the values, perceptions and aspirations of its people and knowing this helps us to gain a better understanding of each other. As we begin to appreciate the strengths of other communities we are able to identify with their aspirations and empathise with their problems. In doing so we can develop a true sense of nationhood and national pride.

East African countries including Kenya, Uganda and Tanzania are of very recent origin. Kenya, for example, created by the British colonialists, became first known as 'Kenia' in 1920. South Asians from the Indian sub-continent have had trade links with the East African Coast for at least 2000 years, if not more. Their permanent settlement extending into the hinterland can be traced back to two centuries. In the case of my own country, Kenya, they form an integral part of the mosaic of the forty-four ethnic communities that make up the Kenyan nation. Notwithstanding this historical reality, other Kenyans often regard South Asians as 'foreigners who belong elsewhere'. The reasons for this are several and include the distinctive culture of the South Asians and their penchant to isolate themselves socially; a trend exaggerated by their political vulnerability. Most crucial, in my opinion, is the absence of a progressive national policy aimed at true nation building. For want of the latter, Kenyans have yet to develop a significant national identity. In Kenya,, it was only in 1974 that the first attempt was made to restructure the literature syllabus in schools when the study of African and black experience was made central to the discipline. Since then much research and writing has been done to promote and popularise the oral literature of the indigenous Kenyan communities.

This book by the Kirmanis is the first attempt to portray the oral literature of East African South Asians. (The migrants from the Indian sub-continent spread out into East Africa and beyond and hence the collection of material in this book is relevant to all areas of the region.) In doing so they have made two major contributions. One is that they have rejuvenated the cultural roots of the South Asians and given parents a hitherto unavailable reference book for story telling and dramatisation for their children.

Second is that teachers can now include South Asian folklore in their oral literature lessons. By so doing they will create better inter-communal understanding and empathy and help to bring East Africa's South Asians closer to the mainstream.

The historical narrative in the introduction clarifies the origins and ultimate settlement of this ethnic group. It is generally little known how the South Asian migrants travelled from the Indian sub-continent to East Africa, the hardships they suffered, the family separations they endured and the struggles they underwent to survive. The song 'In Memoriam' and the experiences of the author's own mother and others are poignant descriptions of those sea faring times.

Travelling by road or rail between Mombasa and Nairobi, Kenyans of all beliefs and social rank stop at the mosque in Mackinnon to pay their respects. Yet how many of them know the story of Sayyed Pir Baghali Shah, the revered saint whose mausoleum it actually is? Readers will find this and other stories informative and meaningful.

I am struck by the importance given to stories involving animals, a very major component of oral literature in East Africa. Of particular note is the close interaction between humans and animals. The use of animal characteristics to highlight human traits is a popular tool for the socialisation of children and is common to all ethnic communities in our region. The timidity of the rabbit, the wisdom of the toad, the intelligence of the jackal and the cunningness of the monkey are just some of many examples. Fables such as 'How the Monkey Got a Red Bottom' and 'The Beasts Who Boasted' are lessons in morality and interesting comparisons can be made in the way different communities view their animals.

South Asian cultural customs and traditions are virtually unknown outside the community. This book will assist the reader to get an insight into South Asian attitudes to, and the practice of, a whole range of landmarks in a person's life. Some of the events are birth, marriage and death as well as religious festivals, the belief in destiny and philosophical arguments between 'fate' versus 'struggle'. Issues such as circumcision and the naming of babies as described are of particular interest to all East Africans. A look at the dowry system in marriage would have been useful.

The value system incorporated in the book is one held by people all over East Africa. It includes the power of prayer and the triumph of good versus evil, truth over falsification. Respect for elders, justice and fair play and basic humanity are some of the others. The book will thus be an additional asset to teachers in their goal of inculcating these values in a child's learning.

The riddles and proverbs are fascinating; one of them says: 'Time flies, words last.' How true!

The authors must be congratulated for their concern in making the book both easily readable as well as a tool for learning. The blend of oral literature originating from the Indian sub-continent and that with its roots in East Africa is skilfully done. The inclusion of some of the passages in their original language gives authenticity and will be of interest to both the speakers of the dialect as well as those interested in further research.

The book will also bridge a major hiatus in the teaching of oral literature in our schools. It should also give impetus to further research into the rich and varied cultural experiences of East Africa's South Asians. Of special concern is the impact of the book on inter-ethnic understanding and interaction. I have no doubt that this book will go a long way in making the question *'Kwenu ni wapi?* (Where is your home?' redundant.

Zarina Patel
FEBRUARY 2002.

PREFACE

Traditions may be passed on orally from one generation to another. Some of these traditions are preserved while others die out over time. The subject of Oral Literature attracts students and scholars from different cultures, especially among Africans, who themselves are inheritors of rich oral traditions. Oral Literature plays an important role in understanding how values and traditions are passed on in a certain community. It helps us to understand why people behave the way they do. This was observed by one of the authors, Dr. Mubina Hassanali Kirmani when she taught Oral Literature in secondary schools in Kenya. Studying Oral Literature exposed students to a wealth of traditions, provoked curiosity about others, and provided better appreciation of people from diverse cultural backgrounds.

This book covers a part of the Indian oral tradition as passed on and preserved in East Africa. It is an effort to preserve what has been passed on for generations among the Indians who settled in East Africa at the turn of the 19th century. At best, it offers a cursory glance at some of the genres of Indian literature. In no way does it claim to capture the depth and diversity of oral traditions offered from each of the Indian communities settled in East Africa. However, it is hoped that the book will help readers to learn and appreciate some of the values and traditions of the Indians. We hope that it will inspire the readers to dig deeper into their own cultures and share their findings with others for enrichment and to foster closer understanding among individuals and communities.

Organisation

This book is divided into six chapters. Chapter One gives the historical origins of the Indians, the social and economic organisation of their communities and their patterns of migration and settlement in East Africa.

Chapter Two examines the dominant features and style of Indian literature as it is preserved in East Africa. It discusses the social setting within which these traditions are transmitted, the role of the artist, and the various symbols, images and figures of speech used to enrich oral discourse.

The subsequent chapters examine each of the four main genres of Indian oral literature in detail. There are examples of narratives given under the various sub-genres: myths, legends, animal tales, moral stories, and tales of wisdom and wit.

Riddles are classified under categories such as cosmology and the physical universe, plants, fruits and vegetables, living creatures, parts of the human body, inanimate objects, and wisdom.

Chapter Five presents proverbs, grouped under the following headings: Proverbs on the power of the tongue, domestic matters, money and wealth, and land and cultivation. There are also proverbs on friendship and human character such as arrogance and foolishness. Included also are proverbs on education and knowledge, and on wisdom.

In the final chapter, dealing with songs, examples are given covering the various sub-genres, including children's songs, and songs for birth, love, marriage, work, journeys by sea, and songs for dance and during times of death.

Sources of material

Most of the material recorded in this book was collected between 1983 and 2001 from various members of Indian communities who migrated from Gujerat, Goa, Punjab and Sindh. Some of the narratives, riddles, proverbs, and songs included are also from the authors' childhood repertoire. Sometimes, material collected had to be verified, substantiated from more than one source, and details cross-referenced with literary works on the culture and traditions of the people who originated from various places in India.

The versions of oral forms included in this book may vary from the versions some of the Indian students may have encountered. This is not unusual because information passed on orally is likely to change from one retelling to another. Students are encouraged to discuss these variations and, where possible, give their own interpretations.

Language

Most Asians in East Africa come from different regions of India and speak different languages. The authors have tried to give examples in Gujerati, Sindhi, Punjabi, Cutchi, Hindi and Konkani. However, since most of the Indian population that migrated to East Africa was from Gujerat, a great number of examples is in Gujerati. We found during the course of our work that Narratives, Proverbs and Riddles are often remarkably the same although occurring in different Indian languages. The authors settled for the most succinct and apt translation irrespective of the original languages in which the genres occurred. These translations are appropriately acknowledged in the chapter notes. Where appropriate, explanations are also included.

Instead of using the Sanskrit-based script, the authors have used Roman letters to facilitate reading by students of non-Indian origin.

It is beyond the scope of this book to get into the complex linguistic aspects of the various languages. However, efforts have been made to distinguish some of the sounds that are unique to Sanskrit-based languages, such as the front palatal sound [tʃ] which is represented with 'ch' in the text, back palatal sound [t] represented by 't' and the rolled sound [∂r] represented by 'r' in the text. Those interested in learning the correct pronunciation may wish to consult with speakers of Indian languages.

•

ACKNOWLEDGEMENTS

This book has benefited from direct and indirect contributions of many individuals. Among these are teachers and scholars such as Professors Okot p'Bitek, Joe De Graft, Taban lo Liyong, David Rubadiri, John Ruganda, and Jared Okungu who have been a great inspiration for this work. We also wish to thank Cynthia Salvadori for allowing us to use the materials from her books, *We Came in Dhows* and *Through Open Doors: A View of Asian Cultures in Kenya*. We are indebted to Mr Madhubhai Patel for his generosity with songs from his book, *Folksongs of South Gujerat,* and to Prof R.C. Mehta from the India Musicological Society. We are equally indebted to Zarina Patel for her critical insights and support on this project.

We are also greatly appreciative of the help provided by the members of various Indian communities in East Africa and outside who generously supported our work by providing ideas, advice, clarification and words of encouragement. We collected from many of them the wealth of narratives, proverbs, songs, and riddles included in this book. Without their support, this work would not have been possible. We wish to extend our appreciation to them all, and particularly to the following individuals:

Ms Zubeda Abbas, Ms Batulbai Anwar, Ms Kokab Arif, Dr Ali Asani, Judge Bandari, Mrs Rematbai Dada, Mrs Sufurabai Dada, Ms Noorbanu Damji, Ms Zarina Diboo, Mrs Bilkis Dossaji, the late Mr Fidahusein Dossaji, Ms Joan D'Souza, Mr Suarez D'Souza, Mrs Krishna Dudani, Dr Niranjan Dudani, Mr Abbas Fidali, Ms Farhat Essajee, Ms Fatima Essajee, Ms Shirin Essajee, Mr Soul Singh Gill, Mrs Sugrabai Gulamabbas, Mrs Asmabai Hassanali, Ms Bilkis Hassanali, Mr Burhan Hassanali, the late Mr Mohamedali Hassanali, the late Mr Murtaza Hassanali, Ms Tahera M.A. Jaffer, Ms Razia Jiwaji, Mrs Rubabai Kaderali, Mrs Rubabai Kapasi, Mr Abid Karimbhai, Mrs Sakina Karimbhai, Mr Issa Kediwalla, the late Mrs Zeni Anver Khandwala, Mr Kassim Esmail Khemisa, Mrs Zainabai Kirefu, Mr Ataullah

Kirmani, the late Mrs Zahra Kirmani, Mr Lalji Laxmikant, Ms Maria Makda, Mrs Fatima Merali, Mr Nazim Mitha, Mrs Aisha Mohammed, Mrs Piroja Mojgani, Mrs Aban Noor, Mr Harbans Singh Noor, Mr K.R. Paroo, Ms Bhanuben Patel, Ms Ila Patel, Ms Kantaben Patel, Ms Parvati Patel, Ms Priti Patel, Ms Saroj Patel, Ms Asmabai Patwa, the late Mrs Sakina Podawalla, Ms Champa Shah, Ms. Ramila Shah, Mr Ajaib Singh, Mr Son Singh, Mrs Shirinbai Sukhadwalla, Mrs Safiyabai Sukhadwalla, Ms Shamim Terai, Ms Manjula Vaghela, Ms Bilkis Waliji, and Mrs Zulekhabai Yamani.

We are grateful to our parents and grandparents for making us aware of our cultural heritage and to our children Nabeel, Muneer and Rasmia for their receptiveness to their culture and traditions.

To all of you, we extend our deepest gratitude.

Chapter One

SOCIO-CULTURAL BACKGROUND

Historical background

The Indians of East Africa, often known as the Asians[1], have their roots in India, across the Indian Ocean. It is sometimes thought that the Indian immigration into East Africa resulted entirely from the building of the Kenya-Uganda railway. In fact, small numbers of Indians had lived in the coastal regions of East Africa for centuries, arriving long before the days of European settlement.

One of the earliest recorded accounts, by Periplus of the Erythean Sea, circa AD 801, mentions Indian as well as Arab ships trading along the East African coast. A Chinese geographical work, dating from the 13th century AD, mentions Gujerati settlement in the same area.[2] There are reports of trading between the west coast of India, comprising Kutch, Surat, Gujerat, Damao, Diu, and Porbander, and the east coast of Africa in the 14th century. This trade continued into later centuries.[3]

Duarte Barbosa, during his visit to Mombasa in 1512, found many ships from the "great kingdom of Cambay", an important seaport of Gujerat. These merchants of Cambay had established a flourishing trade in silk, cotton cloth, and foodstuffs bartered for ivory, wax and gold. The trading connections therefore provide a very plausible answer to the question of why Indians later settled in East Africa. The successful trade drew many people from India to East Africa.

There are other examples noted of Indo-Africa connections. An Indian sailor piloted Vasco da Gama across the Indian Ocean in 1498. The Mogul emperor, Aurungzeb, employed an African admiral in Bombay. The Nizam of Hyderabad, a Muslim ruler in southern India, had a personal African guard during the same era.[4]

1

The British desire for effective control of the Nile waters and the threat of German rivalry created a need for the British to build a railway to connect Lake Victoria to the Indian Ocean at Mombasa. Over 32,000 Indian labourers were employed. The first batch of 350 arrived in Mombasa in 1896. The Indian Government stipulated that each labourer should be allowed to remain in East Africa, if he wished to, at the end of the contract. Most of them returned home after their contract but 6,000 decided to accept the offer to remain in East Africa.

Some of the hazards of construction work during the building of the railway were malaria, dysentery, scurvy, ulcers, and jiggers. Half of the work force was often on the sick list but these were not the only hazards.

In 1898, when the line had penetrated about 100 miles upcountry, at Tsavo, man-eating lions began to terrorise the labourer camps. The labourers were many times reported asserting that it was absolutely useless to shoot the lions since they were not real animals at all, but devils in lions' shape.[5]

Many tales have been passed on about the confrontation of the Indian labourers with the man-eaters of Tsavo. One tale is about two men puffing the *hukka*, a water-smoking pipe. A lion suddenly grabbed one of them and dragged him away. He shouted to the one left behind to make sure that the *hukka*, his only possession, reached his wife. There is another tale of a man once travelling on a donkey with a bundle of kerosene tins hanging on each side of the donkey. The lion jumped at the donkey, and its paws got snared in the tins. The noise of the tins scared off the lion. Both the traveller and the donkey were saved. Then there is a story about the fourteen labourers who were resting in a tent when a lion attacked. Instead of grabbing one of the labourers, the lion got hold of a bag of rice, and groaned in anger at his foolishness.

One of the better known stories though is that of Sayyed Baghali Shah, who is also referred to sometimes as Pir Baghali. He was known to have extra-ordinary spiritual powers. The story behind this legendary figure narrated below is by the late Ikram Hassan.[6] There are also other versions of this story and one version is included in the chapter on narratives. Pir Baghali worked as a labourer on the railway line. He was an honest and a hardworking man. He was always helpful to the needy and was kind to both people and animals. He was known to be strong and athletic, and could run fast enough to catch a peacock or a vulture before it could fly away. Once he caught a running cat that had devoured his cockerel. He was known to be religious and observed his daily prayers. It is said that during construction of the railway, the *kerai* or the vessel filled with concrete and sand which the workers usually carried on their heads, floated a few inches above his head. Pir Baghali was a pious man. It was said that through his prayers, he could help keep the wild animals away and thus keep the labourers' camp safe. When he died, he was buried next to the railway line on Mackinnon Road. A mausoleum has been built there in his memory. Till today many travellers, regardless of whether they are Hindus, Muslims, Sikhs or Christians, stop by his graveside to pay their respects, give offerings and pray for their safe journeys. People say that they arrive safely at their destinations because they had stopped at Pir Bhaghali's graveside. The trains running on the railway line he helped built customarily slow down at Mackinnon Road to pay tribute to this legend.

One other story from the time of the building of the railway is that of Abdul Hamid, known as "Simba Mbili"[7] or "Two Lions." Abdul Hamid came to Kenya around 1890. He had come to work as an inspector on the railway. He had great hunting skills and hunted lions up and down the railway line. Once, when he was stationed at Voi-Ulu, he and his companions saw some lions crossing ahead of them. Abdul Hamid and his group quietly positioned themselves behind a ridge. Abdul Hamid had his .303 rifle. He aimed and shot dead 10 lions. His last bullet killed two lions, for it went right through one and hit another on its neck. And that is how he earned his name "Simba Mbili" . Later, Abdul built a hotel on a plot given to him by the government in Mtito Andei. He called it, Simba Mbili Hotel.

By the end of the 19th century, after the railway was completed, the people in India thought of Africa as a land of economic opportunity. Witness, for example, the slogan, *"Bas chalo Africa!"*[8] which translates into, "Stop! (leave everything) and let us go to Africa!" A call to the courageous spirit of the pioneer and an invitation for better living conditions can be further captured in the following Gujerati proverbs:

Fareh teh chareh.
A person who roams (or travels) advances (to greener pastures).

Bandhyo manas bhuke mareh.
A person tied to one place dies hungry.

The adventurous, along with the others, sailed across the Indian Ocean mainly from Gujerat (comprising Gujerat proper, Cutch, Kathiawar and Surat), Punjab, Sindh, and Goa, to East Africa. At the turn of the 19th century, Asians began their society in East Africa within the context of the British rule while their own country, India was also under colonial rule.

3

Migration and Early Settlement

The migration of Asians, besides their very early presence on the African Coast as discussed earlier, came in two phases. The early group of pioneers settled from 1810 onwards. The later migrants settled after the completion of the railway in 1902. The same factors caused the migration of both groups. The migrants had a spirit of adventure and a willing enthusiasm to go forth and accept hardship with hope for a better life on the other side of the ocean.

Many Asians set off in dhows from Cutch, Mandvi and Bombay to cross the vast and often dangerous ocean. Sometimes, the men sailed first, leaving women and children behind. Often, families were separated for long periods before being reunited. The Badalas, who were seafarers skilled in sailing, played an important role in transporting the Bhatias, Bohoras, Lohanas, Sikhs, Parsis, Ithna' asheris, Memons, Ismailis and many other Indian communities to the East African coast. The journey could take 20 to 30 days.

Often, because of rough seas, the dhows would be wrecked and lost at sea. Many stories have been narrated about these perilous sea adventures. One such story comes from one of the authors' mother, Asmabai Hassanali.

Asmabai had a six-month-old child, Murtaza, when in 1945, she set sail in a dhow from Bombay to rejoin her husband, Mohammedali Hassanali. The journey took nearly 40 days. The men stayed on the deck while the women remained below, occasionally coming for fresh air or to use the toilet. For the first few days, the weather was fine, and then the wind stopped. The dhow hardly moved for the following six days. One of the passengers had annoyed the crew and they wanted to throw him into the sea. Only after much pleading from some of the travellers was the passenger's life saved. Asmabai Hassanali describes it as a long and treacherous journey, which seemed unending. Finally, when the dhow docked in Mombasa, most of the travellers could hardly walk after sitting for so long in such cramped conditions.

The stories of such journeys taken by Asians have been well documented by Cynthia Salvadori in her book, *We Came in Dhows*. There is, for example, the story by Essak Abdul Rehma Kana, "Adrift on a Dhow".[9] He is reported to have come to Africa with his mother in one of the three dhows that set off from Cutch. Each dhow carried 40-odd passengers, including a cargo of cement. It took them two months and ten days to complete the journey. It was between June and July, the worst monsoon season. For the first fifteen days, the weather was fine. Then it suddenly changed and within half an hour, a storm built up. The *nakhoda* (captain) of each dhow had the crew change the sails from the big to the small ones. At nightfall, the dhows were separated.

Although the storm subsided, the sky remained grey for the next ten days. The travellers had no idea where they were heading. There were no radars or other navigational instruments. It began raining, and there was fear that the cement would get wet and heavy, adding to the risks of drowning. The cement bags were thrown overboard. The dhow was leaking and the water had to be pumped out.

All the men and crew helped to save the dhow. There was no sight of land. After a week of calm weather, the wind came up. The captain reckoned that they were off the coast of South Africa. So they turned around and headed back north. On the way, they passed two big cargo ships and asked for help, but received none.

After five days, one of the passengers was finishing his early morning prayers. As he turned his head to the right and then left,[10] he saw something like a rock in the distance. He shouted to the captain. The captain looked through his binoculars and saw the island of Zanzibar. They anchored at Port Chaka and got meat, vegetables and water. Essak Abdul Rehman telegraphed his family in Mombasa of their safe arrival. His family had been extremely worried. Later, all three dhows arrived safely in Mombasa. Essak's mother never recovered from the voyage. Her knees were cramped and her legs were greatly affected from long hours of sitting in wet conditions. She could not walk properly again after the voyage.

There is also the story by Karsonbhai Premji Ganji Bhudia[11] of Mombasa. His grandfather had come in a dhow in 1895. Half a century later, Karsonbhai himself came to Mombasa as a youngster. He had gone back to India to visit his family and returned in a dhow, starting off from Mandvi Port. Eleven dhows departed with the north-westerly winds. The dhows set sail at 4 o'clock in the morning.

The men slept outside as it was hot inside. In case of rain, they took shelter under the canvas. Food consisted of rice, vegetables and *chapatis* made from wheat flour. The food was strictly rationed. In the morning, people bathed in seawater brought up in buckets with ropes. The toilet was a platform of about four square feet with a hole in the centre and a low railing around it. During the daytime, people played cards and read.

After the 23rd day, there was a big storm. It was a terrifying experience. Some travellers started praying while others cried, thinking this was their

5

end. The crew managed to repair the sail. After the storm, every passenger helped to remove the water that had flooded into the dhow. The voyage had taken 28 days. Out of 11 dhows that had left Mandvi, three had disappeared, presumably sunk. Many such stories about these dangerous journeys from India to east coast of Africa have been told in the narratives, poems and songs. The following poem, composed in November 1944, is an example.

In Memoriam

"My mother was snatched at too early an age
My father soon followed that same old stage
And left us three brothers quite helpless, alone
To bear the yoke that they had borne
My mother's death took place at home
Where all of us did weep and mourn
But my father's was a death at sea.
It tore our hearts and orphaned three!

My dad and step-mum and children three
Was sailing to Africa full of glee;
He smiling said, 'I'll come back soon,'
But we knew not death would call so soon.
So sudden God's summons, so quick the deep sea
Did swallow them all, O Destiny,
No time to say farewell, no time to say 'wait'
Death's cold gatekeeper had opened the gate!"[12]

The long and often arduous journeys at sea had to be made somewhat more tolerable. Songs often played an important role in breaking the monotony of the sea and helping sailors to reduce the drudgery of their work. In the examples below, provided by Madhubhai Patel in his book, *Folksongs of South Gujerat*, the soloist leads and the rest of the crew repeat a verse to form a rhythmic beat. More examples of songs are provided in Chapter Six.

Salavo, Salavo

Salavo, Salavo	*Zalla Zumala Heyee*
Heyee vana mali,	*Zalla Zumala Heyee*
Heyee mali veli,	*Zalla Zumala Heyee*
Heyee veli ni,	*Zalla Zumala Heyee*
Heyee chalva lagi,	*Zalla Zumala Heyee*
Heyee dariyey zolan,	*Zalla Zumala Heyee*
Heyee khati chali.	*Zalla Zumala Heyee.*

Sail On, Sail On

Sail, sail on,	*Zalla Zumala Heyee*
Here is my boat,	*Zalla Zumala Heyee*
Her name is Veli,	*Zalla Zumala Heyee*
Veli is my queen,	*Zalla Zumala Heyee*
She sails on the sea,	*Zalla Zumala Heyee*
Swinging to and fro,	*Zalla Zumala Heyee*
Here goes my queen,	*Zalla Zumala Heyee*
Sailing on the sea.	*Zalla Zumala Heyee.*[13]

The migration from India to East Africa separated many families. While men left homes to seek a better future for their families, their spouses were left alone to fend for the households back in India. The following two songs demonstrate the pain of parting as voiced by women left behind.

Wine of Life

While the wine of life overflows the bottle,
My husband has gone to a farther land
Leaving me all alone and deserted.

Who will chat with me?
Who will bathe in the house?
Who will dine with me?
Who will play games with me?

7

Who will swing with me?
Who will sleep with me on my bed?

When the wine of life overflows the bottle?[14]

Odhava, Pranjivan Kyarey Aveshey?

Odhavan, Pranajivana kyarey avashey?
Sachun kahoney mara Shyama,
Sachun kahoney mara Shyama,
Odhava, Vranda tey hanihan vana visey,
Vhaley ramadya rasa, vhaley ladavya Idaa;
Odhava tey rey divasa kyarey avashey?
Odhava, satun sejadi ninder nahi avey,
Rotan rajani viti jai rotan rajani viti jai;
Odhava, Pranajivana kyarey avashey?
Odhava, nathi rey sukati mari ankadi,
Amaney kidhan rey nirasha, vhaley kidhan nirash;
Odhava, Pranajivana kyarey avashey?

Please Tell Me When Shall My Beloved Come?

Please tell me when shall my beloved come?
Tell me the truth when will he come?
Tell me the truth when will he come?
He called me, fondled me.
And played *rasa* with me.
I have no sleep in my bed,
And pass the night sleepless and weeping.
O, tell me when shall my beloved come? [15]

Socio-economic and political organisation

The first settlers either rented or built crude houses with mud walls and iron roofs. There were no medical facilities and no organised community. In spite of adverse conditions, the first migrants found hope in this new land. The later migrants were more practical perhaps, and certainly had more impulse to establish economic stability and a social order. This latter group came, and its members stayed and founded a community.

A few of the pioneers penetrated the mainland even before the advent of the railway in 1895. A leading merchant, Allidina Visram, established trading posts in Uganda 20 years before the railway reached Lake Victoria. Two other traders, Adamjee Alibhoy and M.G. Puri, were well established in Machakos, about 40 miles from Nairobi.

Already, the pattern was being established which was to characterise Indian life in East Africa, one in which commercial initiative was a dominant feature.

In addition to the Asian economic initiative and success, which is well-recognised, the Asians also contributed to the political and social life of East Africa. The African nationalist Harry Thuku, in his autobiography, talks about his interactions with Asians to help confront the colonial rule: "We had many friends among influential Indians —Mangal Dass, Shamsud Deen, Jeevanjee, Suleiman Virjee and others."[16] The pioneer, Alibhai Mulla Jeevanjee, for example, actively participated in politics and launched the first non-white media, the *African Standard* in 1902.[17] Lila Patel, who had studied in Mahatma Gandhi's *Ashram* in Gujerat, actively participated in the Mau Mau war of liberation in Kenya,[18] while P.G. Pinto, a Goan Indian, helped in re-organising the East African Labour Trade Union.[19]

When the railway was completed, most Indians returned to India. Later, Indians arrived independently as *dukawallas* or traders, artisans and professionals. Many maintained the trade or skills passed on for generations in India. In East Africa, therefore, we still have Indian goldsmiths, shoemakers, tailors and launders. Since they came from different parts of India, they brought with them different traditions. They settled and established their own communities. Some of these are Patels, Shahs, Arya Samajis, Lohanas, Sikhs, Bohoras, Ithna' ashris, Ismailis, Memons, Parsis, Sindhis and Goans.

The religions they brought were Hinduism, Islam, Sikhism, Jainism, Christianity and Zoroastrianism. They brought with them their languages such as Gujerati, Cutchi, Punjabi and Konkani. Through family and communal efforts, they have passed on their rich cultural heritage to their children, and to their great grand children. This is how, despite decades of settlement in East Africa, many Indians speak the same tongue their ancestors spoke, eat the same kinds of food their ancestors ate, wear the same type of clothes their ancestors wore, and have maintained the identity their ancestors passed on.

This is also why the oral literature of these translocated Indians clearly reflects that of their origins.

Cultural background

Rites of passage

Birth

Birth is an important event in the homes of East African Asians. The mother-to-be normally goes to her mother's home to deliver, especially if it is her first pregnancy. In earlier days, it was common for women to deliver babies at home with the help of traditionally trained midwives. This has changed and hospitals are now preferred to ensure proper medical care, especially in case of an emergency.

After giving birth, the woman is often required to stay indoors for a certain period. In some communities, the mother stays indoors for 40 days. During this time, she is expected to fully rest and is cared for and fed rich foods such as *Gor paapri* made of pure ghee (calcified butter), brown sugar, nuts and other rich ingredients which are believed to help her regain her strength.

The newly born baby is cuddled and looked after by the grandparents and other relatives. Often, some *kaajal* made of black soot and oil is applied at the back of the ear, or on the sole of the baby's feet to protect it from evil. Sometimes, sacred threads or talismans are tied to its hand or neck for the same purpose.

Naming

The naming ceremony, known as *chahtthi* in Gujerati, is often held six days after birth. Names may be selected from the holy books such as the *Qur'an* or the *Bhagavad Gita*. Children may also be named after religious leaders such as Mohammed, Ali or Fatima, amongst Muslims, and Ram, Laxman or Parvati among Hindus. Sometimes names are given to signify certain meanings such as *Shabnam* (morning dew), or *Kiran* (rays of the sun). Children may also be named after an ancestor. Selecting a name is considered an important duty since it is thought that the child will grow to have the characteristics associated with the name or the person the child is named after. These characteristics also provide an ideal for the child to live up to.

The naming ceremony may vary from community to community. Among some Muslim communities, a close relative, such as a paternal aunt or uncle declares the name. Prayers are whispered into the baby's ears, followed by whispering the child's name in his or her ear three times, such as: "Your name is Fatima." After, the name is announced to other relatives and friends, it is followed by the serving of *mithai* or sweet confectionaries.

In the Sikh community, naming is done by opening the Sikh holy book, *Granth Saheb*, in a *Gurdwara* or at home and a name beginning with the first letter of the first word on the page on the left hand side is picked. If there are more children to be named, then the words following the first are used.

Shaving

The ceremony of shaving the birth hair is an important event amongst some Indian communities of Muslim, Hindu and Jain persuasion. The Muslims call the ceremony *Akika* while Hindus call it *Choodhakarma*. It is generally considered as a sacrifice for the goddess, *Mataji*. The period at which it occurs can vary from one community to another. The birth hair is considered "impure." The hair is removed and either thrown into the sea or buried. Sometimes the hair is weighed and money or valuables equivalent to its weight given out to charity. The baby's bald, shaved head may be covered with saffron, diluted in water. Amongst Muslims, a goat is often sacrificed and the meat shared among relatives and friends.

According to Sikh religious beliefs, both men and women must preserve their hair and never cut it or shave it. Therefore, there is no shaving ceremony in the Sikh community.

Circumcision

Circumcision is a religious obligation for Muslim boys. It is usually performed in infancy or by the age of five in some sects. The earlier practice was for boys to be circumcised at home. The *hajjam* or circumciser visited homes with the *sajyo* or a "sharp knife" and performed the operation. The current practice is to have infants circumcised in hospital soon after birth. In some Muslim sects, circumcision is considered a festive occasion. New and bright clothes are made for the boy and sweets are distributed to family and friends. The other Indian communities such as the Hindu, Parsi, Jain, Arya Samaji and Sikh do not practise the custom.

Marriage

Cradle marriages

The Hindu practice of some parents arranging cradle marriages between their children still survived among the settler Indians in East Africa for a while. An agreement between parents and families committed infants or young children to marriage. The marriage was consummated when the children reached puberty. The practice is no longer known to exist in East Africa.

Arranged marriages

In most Asian communities in East Africa, parents and families choose a life partner for their son or daughter. During earlier times, the suitors hardly had any say in the matter and, in fact, saw one another for the first time on their wedding day.

In later times, photographs could be exchanged so that the girl and boy would have an idea how the future partner looked. In today's arranged marriages, the girl and boy may meet at least once. The suitors may, and mostly do, have some say in the matter. When choosing a husband for their daughter, parents usually pay attention to the boy's character, education, profession, economic status, and his family background. These factors are used to determine how happy their daughter will be in her marriage. The boy's parents may make a decision based on the girl's beauty, character, disposition, cultural education, and family background.

Marriage ceremonies in most Asian communities in East Africa are colourful and happy occasions. They may last from several days to weeks. Relatives and friends from near and far attend these ceremonies. Varieties of food, especially sweet confectionaries such as *laddoos* and *jalebis* are served. Music often spices up the event.

Special clothes are worn for the occasion. Women wear their beautiful reds, greens and yellows to add colour to this event.

The bride is most attractively dressed. The bridal dress may vary from community to community but the *saree,* the long traditional dress, is generally preferred.

Before the final ceremony, the bride's body is adorned with home-made beauty aids. Some communities use *pithi* made from gram flour, tumeric powder and special scents. The *pithi* is applied over the bride's skin and later washed, making her skin look clear and smooth. Her *saree* may be heavily embroidered in gold or silver. She is usually adorned with gold ornaments such as rings, necklaces, bangles, anklets and hair decorations. Her hands are decorated with designs made from *mehndi* or what is also known as *hennah*, made from special leaves that give a bright-red orange colour to the hands. Hindu brides will have a *tilak* on the forehead, and in addition, some very finely drawn colourful patterns decorating the face. Bride and groom are in most communities often garlanded with flowers.

The Hindu wedding ceremony, called *lagan*, takes place around the fire and is conducted by the *pundit* or priest. Prayers are recited and vows exchanged. The couple needs to walk seven times round the fire before they are considered man and wife.

Among Muslims, the religious ceremony is called *nikah*. A religious leader or *Imam*, usually performs the ceremony, but any Muslim with consent from the two families, can conduct it. In some Muslim sects, the woman may be present at the *nikah*, but in others she stays in seclusion and may be represented by her father or a close male relative. The person conducting the ceremony recites prayers and then vows are exchanged. If the bride is secluded, she is asked for her consent before the ceremony can continue. At this time, the woman may refuse the marriage if she so wishes.

After consent has been given, the *nikah* is completed. There is no dowry required by Muslim law. The groom only promises to give his bride an amount of money or property, known as *mahr*, for her financial security.

In the Sikh community, any man or woman may conduct the religious wedding ceremony called *anand karaj*. The holy book, *Guru Granth Saheb*, which is kept on a high pedestal, is opened and a stanza from a hymn is sung. The couple walks around the holy book and exchange vows. This is repeated four times, each with a new stanza of the hymn. One Sikh sect, the Namdhari requires the couple to circle around the fire four times. The use of holy fire during marriage is also common among other Indian communities such as Jains and Zoroastrians.

The bride and her family are sad because tradition requires the girl to leave her home to join her husband in his home. The groom's family is joyous on gaining a new member into their household.

The wedding occasion among Indian communities is often celebrated by songs. Examples of these songs are provided in Chapter Six.

Death

Death marks a solemn period in the community. Death ceremonies are observed differently from community to community. Families and friends gather to console the bereaved family. Special colours, depending on the community, are worn. In some, black or dull-coloured clothes are worn, while in others, the mourners wear white.

The body is prepared in a special way before being taken to its final resting place. Among Muslim communities, the body is bathed with water, and wrapped in a white cloth. Special prayers for the dead are offered before the body is taken to the *qabrestaan*, or cemetery, for burial. Flowers are sometimes laid on the grave. Muslims believe that life on earth is final; depending on one's deeds and faith, God decides on the day of judgment whether one goes to heaven or hell.

Hindus, on the other hand, cremate their dead. The ashes are either scattered into the sea or taken to India to be sprinkled into the holy river, Ganges. Hindus believe that the soul is reincarnated in another human or animal form and will continue to do so depending on the deeds of the person, till the final release or *moksha*.

Sikhs wash the body and clothe it in new white garments, wrap it in a white sheet and then cremate it. The ashes are either taken to Kiratpur in India or sprinkled in any body of flowing water, such as a river. Sikhs also believe in the transmigration of the soul till individual deeds are done exclusively for the sake of one God. The individual soul gets absorbed in God and achieves final release without going through rebirths.

Parsis are traditionally expected to expose the body to vultures, but in East Africa, the body is buried. The family fasts and prays for three days after the death. Commemorative prayers for the dead are held at different times during the year.

Muslims remember the dead periodically with food and prayers in a ceremony known as *fateha*. The widow goes into *Iddat* or seclusion within the confines of her home for a little over four months. The purpose of seclusion is to make sure that any child the widow may have conceived belongs to her late husband. The Hindu wife removes the *tilak* she wore on her forehead to indicate her married status.

There are many stories about the dead. Some Asians, for example, believe that if a person dies in an accident or prematurely before his time, his ghost may float around the world. Also, the dead may come into the dreams of a relative or a friend to inform of certain things that the person could not relate while he or she was alive.

Review questions

1. Name and describe the ceremonies that may take place around a newborn child in your community.

2. Is there a preference for children of a particular gender? If yes, why is this so? What are your views about this?

3. How were marriage partners selected in your community? What are your views about it? Does this practice still exist?

4. Describe how the bride and the groom are beautified for marriage in your community.

5. Name and describe some of the important ceremonies that take place around marriage in your community.

6. Are there any customs that a pregnant woman is expected to observe? Describe those that are commonly observed in your community.

7. Name and describe some of the ceremonies that take place around the dead in your culture.

8. Have you heard of any stories about the dead? Narrate one of them.

Project suggestions

1. Organise a class project where you exhibit bridal clothing from different cultures.

2. Invite an elder or priest in your community to discuss procedures followed during (a) birth; (b) marriage; and (c) death.

3. Invite a group of women from different cultures and have them discuss their experiences of giving birth within the context of their respective cultures.

Chapter Two

STYLE AND PERFORMANCE
OF ORAL LITERATURE

Asians oral literature has special features and characteristics. It can be divided into four main genres, namely narratives, proverbs, riddles and songs. The context and style in which these genres are performed is discussed below.

Performance

The social setting

Many of the traditions of Asians in East Africa have been transmitted orally from generation to generation through informal discourse at home, in social gatherings, or in places of worship.

Stories and riddles are normally narrated at the end of the school or work day, or after a meal when the family is relaxing. Although this tradition is disappearing, especially in nuclear family units, it is still fairly prevalent in extended family systems. Adults are sometimes seen eating betel leaf, called *paan*, and betel nut, or *supari*, and spending time with their children.

Children normally gather around an older relative to hear stories, riddles or jokes. Another important setting where children get exposed to cultural values is in larger gatherings where relatives and friends visit each other or go for picnics. In a business-oriented family, when the shops have been closed, the topic of the evening may revolve around markets and trade. The proverb, *"Eneh laakh na baar hazaar karya,"* (He made twelve thousands out of a hundred thousands), for example, may be quoted when describing someone who foolishly lost money in a trade deal.

Religious myths and legends are told in places of worship by priests, who emphasise the moral aspects of the tale. A good narrator can draw examples from day-to-day behaviour to teach youngsters how to lead a morally acceptable life. Some stories, from the *Ramayana* or *Mahabharata* for example, are acted out in the Hindu communities. These two epics tell the life of the gods, Lord Rama and Lord Krishna.

Religion is central to the culture of Asians and some of the religious events are critical in passing on traditions. Some of the religious festivals of note for Asian Muslims are, for example, *Eid-ul-Adha*, marking the end of the pilgrimage to Mecca, and *Eid-ul-Fitr*, marking the end of the fasting month. *Navjote* is the initiation ceremony for youngsters into the religion among Zoroastrians. The Ismailis celebrate the *Imamate* day when an *Imam* is installed as their religious and community leader. Some of the Hindu festivals include *Diwali*, or festival of lights, and the *Navratri*, during which women and girls gather in temples, homes and social halls for nine nights to sing and do the *Garba Ras* dances. All these festivals provide rich social occasions for learning about communal traditions and values.

The storyteller as an artist

Stories may be told by any individual with a repertoire of folk tales who enjoys being with children. Children are normally quick in knowing a good storyteller within the immediate or extended family. An aunt, uncle or grandparent normally gets selected since he or she spends more time and has patience with children.

Children eagerly gather around him or her to hear the story. A good artist is normally one who can integrate various genres such as songs, riddles and even proverbs, to make the story engaging and interesting. To make the narration lively, the artist may imitate sounds representing different characters, human or animal. He or she may capture the attention and imagination of the audience through vivid descriptions, voice variations and gestures.

The artist may even pose questions during the narration to get the children's help in unfurling the plot of the story. Humour, wit, and suspense are some of the tools a good storyteller may use.

Although the tradition of telling stories in the streets through use of animals such as monkeys and bears still lives on in India, it has not been brought to East Africa. Also, puppet theatres are common in India where certain stories, epics and sagas are voiced out by backstage narrators and played out by puppets. These performances have also not been brought to East Africa, but may be easily introduced with a bit of creativity and increase in interest.

17

Audience participation

Children normally make a great audience for narratives. They participate in religious and social occasions such as births and marriages. They are expected to be good listeners. They circle around an older relative on the floor, sitting with their legs crossed as is done in yoga.

As they eagerly wait to hear the story, they may be asked to run little errands, to bring water for the narrator or ensure that the lights are off in the unused areas of the home. Children normally run these errands at great speed to ensure that the beginning of the narration is not delayed.

In Gujerati-speaking homes, once the narrator has begun the story, children may be heard saying, *"Pachi, pachi"* which means, "And then, and then." This statement may be repeated several times in the course of the story, manifesting the children's curiosity over how the tale will evolve.

In the course of the narration, children may ask questions and show their emotions by laughing, nodding in agreement, or shaking their heads in disagreement, clapping their hands in amazement, and so on.

As soon as the story is over, children are likely to say, *"Biji, biji"* meaning "One more, one more." At this point, the narrator may tell another story or give strict instructions for the children to go to bed.

Children also learn about traditions and values by participating in family and social gatherings. In the presence of adults, children are expected to follow a strict code of behaviour. Showing respect towards adults is very important among Asians. One way to show respect is by being quiet when adults are talking. Such discipline, in fact, becomes an important vehicle for learning cultural values since careful listening skills are developed.

Children hear adults talking about personal experiences, about current events in the community such as marriages, births and deaths, and about domestic affairs and business transactions. Children get to learn both simple and complex uses of language, application of certain imagery and symbolism, and thus gather certain subtle uses of language. By being an attentive audience, they also begin to understand some of the cultural and moral values of the community.

In places of worship, be they temples, mosques or *gurdwaras*, the audience, both young and old, are careful listeners to the moral lessons preached by religious teachers. They take time to reflect on their own actions. Sometimes, sermons may be followed by the congregation singing and reciting religious hymns and prayers for guidance and peace.

Participation in poetry gatherings, known as *mushaira,* is becoming increasingly popular among certain Asian groups. During these occasions, Urdu language is normally used. Urdu, which originated in the northern part of India and is also used in Pakistan, is considered to be the tongue of the cultured. There is an increasing interest in both understanding and learning of this language. Videos of Urdu plays are fast making their way into some homes.

People normally gather in homes or social halls for the poetry or *mushaira* sessions. A whole range of themes is covered. These include love, death, war, domestic feuds and patriotism. Some of the famous Indian Urdu poets, such as Mirza Ghalib, are quoted at these sessions. A person may also create his or her own poem and share it with the group. The following Gujerati poem was presented by Haroon Ahmed on Kenya's Independence Day through a radio programme in 1963.

Kadhi sthar hadhitaan ma rehvu pare che
Na desho paraya vatan pun bane che
Aaj Kenya ne je mukti mali che
Ham vatan sau ma tamne pun e jari che
Hata bedh kala dhoro rango no
E aaj panch rangi praja bane che

Translation[20]

At times we have to reside in foreign lands
But a foreign country can become your motherland
The freedom that Kenya has won today
Is for all wananchi including you
There was discrimination between black and white
Today there is mixing in this nation's society

Performance formulae

There is no rigid way of introducing or ending a story or riddle. However, a common beginning among Gujerati speakers when telling a story are, "*Ek vaar ek hato,*" which means, "At one time there was" or "Long time ago, there was". In Punjabi, "*Bahot dina di gull hey*" may be used which means, "This story is of long time ago." Although stories can have different endings,

19

those for children tend to have a happy ending. The Gujerati tales normally end with, "*Khathu pithu neh raaj kithu*", that is to say that the good character(s) in the story "Ate, drank and lived like a king", or an equivalent expression.

During *mushaira* sessions, participants normally sit on the floor. Whoever has a couplet or a verse to recite begins with a request: "*Arz hey*", which is equivalent to, "I would like to humbly say". The audience normally replies: "*Irshad*," meaning, "Please speak." Through use of imagery, symbolism, and figures of speech, words are put together to convey deep meanings and views about life.

When the poet's recitation is good, the audience responds with, "*Waah, waah*" in appreciation and may add, "*Mukerrar irshad*," meaning, "Please say it again." Normally, the *mushaira* session goes on late into the night and into the early hours of the morning.

Style of oral narratives

The style with which a story is presented depends mostly on the narrator. The adept narrator tailors the presentation to the occasion and the audience. The core of the narrative may remain the same, but the elements in which the core is clothed depend on the occasion. If the story is told to children, it is often dynamically edited to strike out abstract complexities, which children may not understand.

The length of narratives may also vary. Some stories may be told in two nights and may have flashbacks and reminders of the story's beginning. In this way, the audience is constantly reminded of the occasion, which brought about the tale.

Some of the specific events in the narrative may make references to some current events to convey the meaning more clearly and in more practical terms. This is particularly so when certain moral lessons are supposed to be conveyed. Certain points may also be repeated in several ways for emphasis.

The narrator may go through the narrative in a halting fashion to create suspense, so that he or she will motivate the audience to seek further details or continuations. If the narrative is acted out on a stage, such as in the Ram stories, the elements of suspense and surprise may easily be conveyed to the audience. For example, in performed Ram stories, the actor who plays the role of the deer sent by the vicious and demonic Ravana, or the one who acts the monkey god, Hanuman, may enact the situation to surprise the audience, especially children, by sprinting and jumping out from behind the stage.

Humour and wit are used carefully and sparingly to ensure that they do not insult the audience or obscure the message of the story. Sometimes, the content of the story itself may provide wit and humour, as in the stories about Akbar and Birbal. The skill of one character, either human or animal, outwitting the other often forms the basis for such stories.

Figures of speech

A talented artist normally uses symbolism, imagery and other figures of speech to enrich and clarify his story or song. A symbol may be used to represent an abstract idea. In Indian oral literature, a person may be compared to a *gai* or a cow to signify a generous nature, or kindness and gentleness. Phrases such as *"Garib gai jevo che"*, meaning "He is like a poor cow" or *"Allah Mia ni gai,"* meaning "He is like God's cow," describe a person who is kind and tolerant. Another simile close to the above is *"Dharti Mata"*, meaning, "Mother Earth". The earth is often compared to a mother since it selflessly gives and provides sustenance.

Similes such as "Children are like flowers" or metaphors such as "Children are flowers" are commonly used to describe the innocence, beauty and delicate nature of children. Just as the Maasai woman in prayer may ask for long greasy hair to mean a child, [21] a married Hindu woman may ask God for her *tilak* to be preserved on her forehead. This is a request for the long life of her husband. A widow is expected to remove the decoration from her forehead.

Characterisation

Narratives have all kinds of characters, including humans, animals, gods and demons. Human characters take a variety of roles from being poor, rich or loyal, to intelligent, brave, witty or foolish. Similarly, animals are commonly used in narratives to depict various human characteristics. Animals form an important part of Hindu mythology and legend as indicated in the first six stories of Chapter Three.

Animals are present both within the religious context and as beings that represent some of the worldly human traits. The rabbit, for example, is timid as shown in Story 11, and the monkey is cunning as indicated in Story 12. While gods represent good in life, demons are the opposite and represent evil. Both gods and demons are present in myths and legends, as will be noted in Stories 1 to 6 in Chapter 3.

Review questions

1. Based on your own experience, identify some of the social settings in which stories, riddles, proverbs, and songs are passed on in your home or community.

2. Explain some of the ways in which the audience participates in narrative sessions and how they learn some of the traditions within your community from them. Describe the ages and the social status of the participants.

3. List, translate and explain some of the symbols, images and figures of speech used in your community.

Chapter Three

NARRATIVES

Narratives preserved by Asians in East Africa may be classified into several categories. These include myths, legends, historical tales, animal tales, moral stories, wisdom tales and tales of destiny.

Myths

Myths have been defined as narratives about the past and may include explanations of natural phenomena such as creation, birth, and death[22] . Myths may also tell us about the nature of God, sacred beings and divine heroes. This is particularly true of Indian myths. They are said to convey deep truths about nature, cosmology and sacred realities.[23] The narrative below is a creation myth explaining the beginning of life in this world. The three stories after it are tales of origin explaining about Hindu gods and the natural phenomena of the moon and earthquakes.

1. The Beginning of Life in This World

Brahma the creator of the earth was greatly troubled by the way mankind behaved in the world. People were unkind, dishonest, power-hungry, waged war against one another and did evil. The only person who lived a holy and a balanced life was Manu. He was accompanied by seven sages. Manu meditated at the edge of a stream and thought of Brahma for thousands of years.

One day a small fish that was trying to escape from a bigger fish popped out of the stream and begged Manu to save its life. Manu readily helped by taking the fish and placing it in a small container. Soon the fish became too big for the small container and Manu placed it in a bigger container. The fish grew bigger and Manu poured it into a pond. The fish continued growing and Manu carefully placed it in the holy river, Ganges. The river soon became too small for the fish and Manu placed the fish into the ocean. The fish was grateful for Manu's help. It thanked him and warned him about the end of the world.

Brahma wanted to end the world since mankind had greatly displeased him. He wished to begin a new one. He decided to send a huge flood and cover the earth with water. The fish advised Manu and the seven sages to build an ark and carry seeds from every plant.

The whole world soon became one big ocean. Manu and the seven sages remained on the ark while the huge fish towed the ark through the waters for many years till they reached the highest peak of the Himalaya Mountains. There Manu and the seven sages got off.

Soon the big fish announced, "I am God Vishnu, the preserver. Because of your purity and holiness, Manu, I have chosen you to do the work of creation."[24] And then the fish disappeared.

When the waters receded, Manu and the seven sages came down from the mountains. Manu soon began the work of creation. He scattered the seeds and created all the plants, animals, the men, the gods, and the demons.

"And the world in which we live began." [25]

Review questions

1. The myth above is part of a community's search for explanations of the existence and formation of our universe. Can you think of a similar myth from your community?

2. Discuss your myths in class and determine any similarities and differences between those presented.

2. The Creation of Ganesh, the God with an Elephant Head

The God Lord Shiva carries heavy responsibilities of the world. In fact, he is so preoccupied with his work that he is absent for days and months from the side of his consort.

On one such occasion when he was absent for a long time, his wife Parvati got very bored being alone. Now, being a goddess herself, she decided to create a baby to keep her company and to keep her occupied. Once the child was created she decided to call him Ganesh. Oh, how she loved the baby and enjoyed having him. She played with him all the time.

A long time passed. Shiva was still busy and he had not come home yet. In the meantime, the baby began to walk and talk and grew into a fine boy. One day, Parvati decided to take a bath in the river. Because she did not wish her privacy to be disturbed, she asked Ganesh to sit by at a distance and stop anyone who might be coming to the river.

Well, it so happened that Shiva finished his work and returned at that time. He did not find Parvati, so he went looking for her. He looked here and there and everywhere. In the course of his search, he decided to go to the river.

As he approached the river, little Ganesh barred his way and would not budge. That made Shiva extremely angry. In his anger, he cut Ganesh's head off.

Parvati heard a scream and ran out to find what Shiva had done.

"This is the worst crime!" she shouted, "You have killed our only child!"

Shiva was utterly surprised since he did not know that they had a child. Parvati was beside herself with sorrow. She refused to have anything to do with Shiva and insisted that Shiva bring their son back to life.

Shiva loved Parvati dearly, and was willing to do anything to please her. He now had to find a living creature to bring Ganesh's body back to life. Parvati asked him to get the head of the first living creature he found and bring the boy's life back without further delay.

Shiva left immediately and started hunting. The first creature he found was an elephant. He cut the elephant's head off and put it on Ganesh's body and so brought him back to life. Parvati was very happy.

"This child is even more beautiful than before," she said with delight. Shiva agreed. He was already getting fond of their son.

That is how Ganesh got the elephant head. Ganesh is worshipped and greatly loved and he grants success to those who worship him.[26]

Review questions

1. The Hindu myth above explains the origin of the God, Ganesh. Narrate a myth from your community or any other community, which describes the concept of creation.

2. How is the creation myth that you have described different from, or similar to, the creation of the god Ganesh?

3. Why the Moon Appears and Disappears

One night God Ganesh was riding on his rat. On the way, a snake suddenly crossed the path. The rat was shocked and turned suddenly to avoid the snake. Ganesh lost control and tumbled to the ground. The moon and the stars that had been watching from above could not help laughing. Ganesh was very upset at their behaviour. So he removed one of his tusks and threw it at the moon. The world became dark.

The gods were worried and asked Ganesh to forgive the moon. After much pleading from the moon, Ganesh reached up and removed the tusk. But since he was greatly insulted he decided that he would regularly take away the moon's light till it became only a silver line and then give the light back only to take it away again. This is why the moon appears and then disappears.[27]

4. Why the Earth Trembles

The earth rests on the horn of a bull. When the bull gets tired and shifts the weight of the earth from one horn to the other, the earth trembles, resulting in an earthquake. [28]

Review questions

1. The two myths above explain a natural phenomenon about the moon and the earth. Think of a myth from your community which describes the origin of some natural phenomena.

2. Discuss your myths in class and make a list of various natural phenomena. Identify the community from which the myth comes and give a brief description of its origins.

Legends

A legend is a narrative about a historical character or event.[29] Legends within the Indian culture focus on the lives of people who have accomplished great deeds. They are normally narrated in the form of prose or poetry.

Through collective cultural recollection and retelling, the heroes of the tales acquire the status of supernatural beings. As heroes, they are often held up as models of extraordinary power, goodness, devotion, bravery and piety.

One of the modern-day legendary figures of India is Mahatma Gandhi, the great freedom fighter, who led India to independence from the British as did for example, Jomo Kenyatta in Kenya. Gandhi believed in non-violence. He had extraordinary wisdom and spiritual power to unite the people of India against the toughest forces of the British and defeat them.

While legends are normally built around historical characters, the following stories are about Ram and Krishna, each of whom is an incarnation of the Supreme Being. They are legendary figures who exemplify the best in human

26

beings. Ram and Krishna tales are collected in the ancient epics, known as *Ramayana* and the *Mahabharata*.

Story 7 is a different kind of legend based on an unusual, almost heavenly love between a man and a woman during the Mogul rule in India. The story that follows it is a local East African legend based on Pir Baghali, an Indian labourer who participated in the building of the Kenya-Uganda railway and who is believed to have had supernatural powers.

5. The Story of Ram

King Dashrat was the ruler of the great kingdom of Ayodhya. He was a devoted religious man and a kind king. One day while hunting, he mistakenly killed Shravan who was taking his parents for pilgrimage. The parents of Shravan, on losing their son, put a curse on King Dashrat. While the people of Ayodhya enjoyed the just rule of King Dashrat, King Ravan, the leader of demons, ruled Lanka.

Ravan had ten heads and 20 arms. Even the gods could not destroy him, since he had extracted a promise from them that no heavenly being or underground creature would destroy him. The only way they could destroy Ravan was through an *avtar*, a god reborn in the form of man.

King Dashrat had three wives and four sons. The first wife was Kaushaliya and she had one son, Ram. The second wife, Sumitra, had twins — Laxman and Shatrughan. The third wife, Kaykeyi had one son, called Bharat.

The three brothers loved and respected each other. The eldest son, Ram, was an *avtar*, born as a man but with the power of a god. Ram won beautiful Sita's hand in marriage by winning the challenge put forward by her father, King Janak, to string a special heavenly bow.

Ram and Sita were very devoted to one another.

Ram, being the eldest, was heir to the throne. Now, it so happened that King Dashrat's third wife, Kaykeyi, had on one occasion saved the king's life. In gratitude, King Dashrat had promised to grant her any two wishes. Kaykeyi had not yet asked for her wishes.

The time cam to choose the new heir. Now, before King Dashrat passed his throne to Ram, Kaykeyi's scheming maid misguided her into telling King Dashrat that one of her wishes was to have her son, Bharat, succeed to the throne. And her other wish was to have Ram banished into the forest for fourteen years.

King Dashrat was shocked beyond words, but Ram wished his father to keep his word and prepared to leave the next day. As a devoted wife, Sita insisted on joining her husband in the forest. Laxman wished to join them so that he could take care of the couple.

Bharat, who was now to be the new heir, was greatly saddened by his mother's behaviour. He knew the injustice of the situation and promised Ram that he would guard the throne till he returned from the forest. He told his brother, "I will never sit on the throne but will instead place your wooden slippers on the throne, and rule in your name till you return!"

Ram, Sita and Laxman departed as the people of Ayodhya wept. Ram walked barefoot since his slippers lay on the throne. As the years passed, he and his companions walked deeper and deeper south into the forest, towards Lanka. In the thirteenth year, they reached Dandaka Forest, which was filled with demons, ruled by Ravan, the king of Lanka.

Soon, Ravan heard the news that Ram and his companions were close to his kingdom. The vicious, demonic Ravan sent a magical golden deer to capture Sita and to lure Ram and Laxman away from her so that she could be kidnapped. Sita was immediately attracted to the beautiful deer. Failing to catch it herself, she asked Ram to catch it for her.

Ram, assisted by Laxman, tried to capture the deer without success. Suddenly, with great swiftness, the deer jumped away into the woods. Ram told Laxman to look after Sita and made him promise that he would not leave her alone, no matter what happened. Then he went in pursuit of the fleeing golden deer. After a short while, Sita heard a human cry from the woods and believed that Ram was in danger. She persuaded Laxman to go to Ram's aid. Laxman refused to do so, and Sita became frantic about Ram's safety.

Laxman had to break his promise to Ram. He left Sita alone. Ravan saw his opportunity so he kidnapped Sita and carried her off to Lanka in his chariot of the skies.

Ram chased the deer, and finally had to kill it because it was demonic. Realising that he had been tricked, he and Laxman hurried back to Sita, only to find that she had disappeared.

Meanwhile, the vulture king, Jetayu, had detected Ravan's kidnapping of Sita. The giant bird attacked Ravan to rescue Sita but Ravan crippled him. Ram and Laxman approached the bird in its dying moment. It had just enough time to inform them of how Ravan had kidnapped Sita.

In his desperate search and attempt to rescue Sita from the demon Ravan, Ram gained full support from a new powerful ally — the monkey king, Hanuman. Hanuman set out to Lanka. In order that Sita would not take Hanuman for an imposter, Ram gave Hanuman his ring so that she would immediately recognise it.

28

Hanuman, using his supernatural abilities, leapt across the ocean and reached Lanka. He found Sita guarded by Ravan's niece in one of the palace gardens.

Ravan came to see Sita and tried to woo her, but was rudely rebuffed. Ravan got angry and drew out his dagger to kill Sita but was stopped by his niece. Ravan, frustrated, left the garden for his palace. Hanuman approached Sita and gave her Ram's ring. In return, Sita gave Hanuman her hairpin to show Ram that she was still alive and waited for him to rescue her.

Hanuman left and created havoc and commotion in the city. Ravan was furious and prepared his army of giants to fight Hanuman. By now, Ram had joined Hanuman and, together, they were victorious.

Ram joined Sita and they lived happily ever after.

In this narrative, Ram represents the victory of good against evil, which is represented by Ravan.[30]

Review questions

1. The legend above describes the triumph of good over evil. List the good characters and describe the deeds which you consider of good moral value.

2. Discuss a legend from your community, where good conquers evil.

6. Lord Krishna and the Serpent King

In the village where Lord Krishna lived, there were many reports that every time somebody went to bathe in River Yamuna, or even tried to swim across, they were never seen again. Cattle and chickens were disappearing mysteriously around the river.

There was a real panic in the village. Mothers kept their children away from the shore. One day — a very well-built person who was a yogi went to take a bath in the river. As soon as he stepped into the water he felt a tug, so he immediately, with all his strength, swam to the dry land. When he turned around, he noticed that there was a huge serpent with five heads that had been lunging at him.

Now he was sure what had happened to all those people who had disappeared. He immediately went and reported to the village elders.

They had never heard of such a thing, and knew that the only person who could help them get rid of such a menace was Lord Krishna. Lord Krishna was, from a young age, seen as a leader and highly respected by the community. They soon went to him and asked him for help.

29

Lord Krishna took three or four of his friends with him and went into the river. He did this to entice the serpent. As soon as he saw the serpent rising to grab them, he immediately shouted at others to get out of the water, putting himself alone in danger. The villagers yelled at him to leave the river, yet he was so concerned about the welfare of the people that he was ready to put himself in extreme risk in order to save them.

The serpent lunged at him and tried to curl one of its heads around Krishna's legs in order to pull him down. But Lord Krishna was swift and he put his other foot on the serpent's head, and while the serpent was still struggling he reached in and grabbed its other head in his hand, pinching it tightly between his thumb and forefinger. With the other hand, he took the third head and twisted it. The serpent fought hard to free its head, and in its anger and frustration; started to bite Krishna with his two free heads.

Krishna increased his pressure on the heads he was holding till they were destroyed. As the serpent tried to bite him with his remaining heads, Krishna grabbed the heads with his other hand and, with superhuman strength, that he summoned, he completely quashed the heads till the serpent flopped and died. And the people were free of the threat.

Such was the greatness of Krishna.[31]

Review questions

1. The legend above focuses on the bravery of Lord Krishna. Narrate a legend from your community which focuses on bravery.

2. Discuss the legends on bravery in class, paying special attention to how different communities identify acts of bravery.

7. The Legend of Love

The Taj Mahal is a well-known monument in India. It was built by Shah Jehan to demonstrate his great love for a woman. As the legend goes, during the rule of the Mogul emperors in India, every Wednesday the royal court would arrange for an open market, usually outdoors, where the noble families and other selected families would shop. The market was called *Meena Bazaar*. This bazaar was especially arranged so that the ladies of the emperor's household and the royal court could easily move about and enjoy the experience of being in a busy, bustling market.

Shah Jehan, who was emperor Jehangir's son, happened to visit the Meena Bazaar on one of the Wednesdays. Shah Jehan was heir to the throne. As he walked about the stalls in the market and looked at various wares, clothes and ornaments, his eyes fell on one of the young girls standing near one of the stalls. He was totally struck by the beauty of this girl, and felt himself drawn to that stall.

In order to stay there and look at her some more, without making things obvious, he asked her what she was selling. Apparently, she was also attracted to the prince and wanted this game of eyeing back and forth to continue, so she pretended that was was selling a diamond necklace.

She did not know whom she was talking to. She named a price that she thought not even a prince could afford. She said, "This unique necklace is priceless. It is for ten thousand gold coins!"

That indeed was a lot of money, but the person who was inquiring was also a prince. And now that he was so madly attracted to her, he was ready to pay any price for it. So he reached into his sleeve and counted out the money. Soon the girl realised that this was probably a prince. Exchanging the necklace for the gold coins she immediately disappeared into the crowd.

The prince was awestruck with her beauty and was already pining after her. He asked around who the girl was and found out that her name was Arjumand Banu and that she was the daughter of the *wazir* or the prime minister. Arjumand had won the prince's heart and he wanted to marry her.

He went to his father, the emperor, and told him of his wish. The emperor himself, being a poet and a writer, appreciated and understood fully the presence of great love in his son and agreed to his request.

Soon, servants bearing gifts, sweets and clothes were sent to the prime minister's house to ask for the hand of his daughter in marriage to Shah Jehan. Of course she was also attracted to him and willingly consented. The young couple had to wait for two years before they could wed on the date the royal astrologers had fixed. Everything had to be just right for the royal wedding. All kinds of preparations had to be made. Princes and Rajas and their families from all over India had to be invited. Finally, everything was ready. The prince could hardly wait, neither could Arjumand. Of course, during these years, they had secretly exchanged letters and gifts and stolen glances especially at Meena Bazaar.

Finally the wedding took place with a large procession of a fully dressed military and the emperor's personal guard. Jugglers, musicians, acrobats, decorated elephants and horses formed part of the procession. Servants bore gifts of all sorts.

Finally, Arjumand married Shah Jehan and came to the palace. The whole palace was brightened up by her presence. What a beautiful person she was both in her looks and mannerisms. She won everyone's heart, including that of the emperor who gave her the title, *Mumtaz Mahal* or the chosen one of the palace. The love between Shah Jehan and *Mumtaz Mahal* flowered and deepened. People throughout the land used to point to them as an example of true love and devotion.

In course of time, Shah Jehan succeeded his father and became the emperor of India. With a pleasant domestic life, Queen Mumtaz bore him several children. Unfortunately, during one of the births, she died.

The emperor Shah Jehan was beside himself with grief and sorrow. It is said that he closed himself in a room without food or drink for several days. It was only after much pleading from his children and palace staff that Shah Jehan came out of his seclusion. When he came out, the people around him could not believe their eyes.

There was a sudden transformation in him. His hair, which was black, was now white. He walked stooped like an old man whereas he was stout and hearty before his wife died.

Shah Jehan eventually had to deal with the affairs of the empire, but he made up his mind that he would erect a mausoleum for his beloved wife. He wanted to build a monument of such beauty and grandeur that people would admire it and be struck by its beauty and would remember his love for his wife for all time to come. He started the building; planners and builders as well as special craftsmen were brought in from all over the world. The building took many years to complete. It was made in white marble and was studded with precious gems so it twinkled and glowed night and day. Today, the monument, Taj Mahal, stands containing the graves of Mumtaz and Shah Jehan. It is a monument of a man's love for a woman. People are drawn from all over the world to the Taj Mahal in Agra.

It is one of the seven wonders of the world.[32]

Review questions

1. Explain what makes the love between Shah Jehan and Mumtaz Mahal so special.

2. Narrate a legend from your community that focuses on love. In what ways is the love you describe unique or special?

8. Sayyed Pir Baghali Shah

The building of the Kenya-Uganda railway brought many Indians to East Africa to work as labourers, clerks and artisans. Many stories are told about the early Indian settlements and about their long journeys on stormy seas before they reached the East African coast.

Many stories are also told about the initial efforts of pioneer Indian individuals and families as they established themselves, worked on building the railway and started new trade links.

Among these stories is a widely popular tale of an Indian labourer named Pir Baghali. He was a wise old man with spiritual powers. People say that while Pir Baghali worked, the *kerai* or vessel for carrying concrete and sand always remained a few inches above his turbaned head. He was also known to speak and understand the language of animals.

On one occasion, when the working party was around the area of Mackinnon, where the labourers had camped and were clearing the bush, a huge python appeared. It had stretched its fangs and was ready to strike at anyone who dared to approach it. Some of the labourers were ready with their *lathis* or sticks, while one of the Englishmen raised his gun to shoot.

Pir Baghali begged them not to harm the animal. Instead, he asked them to step aside while he knelt down and prayed. He then faced the snake and pleaded, requesting it to leave in peace. The snake stood for a while, poised to attack, but after a while, it gradually backed down and slithered away. Pir Baghali's power of prayer, it is said, also kept the lions away and the labourers in his camp remained safe. When he died, he was buried next to the railway line in Mackinnon in Kenya, and a monument has been built there in his memory.

Today, many travellers on the Mombasa-Nairobi road visit the monument to pay their respects to Pir Baghali, and they say that the train normally slows down and whistles as it passes near Pir Baghali's monument.[33]

Review questions

1. What is special about Pir Baghali that makes him a legend?

2. Narrate a legend from your community which focuses on supernatural powers.

Animal tales

In India, people and animals co-exist peacefully. Cows graze and walk down the village streets without being disturbed, and monkeys play and chatter in the temple gardens.

Certain religious groups believe that it is sinful to kill any living creature, even insects.

To understand further the respect Indians have for all animals, one has only to look at Hindu, Jain or Buddhist temples. The temple walls are often decorated with paintings of animals. In these temples, one also finds sculptures of birds and beasts carved besides those of humans and gods.

In Hindu mythology, the gods are associated with certain animals that act as their vehicles and the gods themselves may also, at times, assume the shape of an animal. Vishnu, the Preserver rides upon Garuda, a man-bird, and, while taking the form of a fish and a boar, saves the earth. Ganesh, the god of success, rides upon a rat and has the head of an elephant. In the folktales, men and beasts not only speak to one another but also slip in and out of each other's worlds and shapes with ease.

In some of the fables, animals act out the truths of ancient folk wisdom, in other tales, they portray certain human characteristics that range from intelligence to foolishness. The first story in this section tells about the wisdom of the toad, the one after it shows the intelligence of the jackals, and Story 11 demonstrates the timidity and the foolishness of a rabbit. Story 12 describes the cunning of the monkey while Story 13 explains how the monkey got a red bottom.

9. The Beasts Who Boasted

Once, an elephant, a lion, a fox, and a peacock were said to have met at a pond in the forest.

The elephant began flapping its huge ears, looked down at the others from his great height and blew his trumpet.

"You have to agree that I am the strongest of all the beasts. With my long tusks, I can tear through the thickest forest. Trees are like little twigs to me," he trumpeted.

"You may be strong," roared the lion, "but nothing compares to my bravery. It is because I am brave that I am the king of the forest."

"Not at all. Brains are more important than bravery and mere strength," said the fox. "I live extremely well just by my wits."

"To be able to crash through the woods, or leap into thin air, or sneak into the chicken yard is worthless compared to beauty," said the peacock. He demonstrated this by preening his colourful feathers in a dance. All this while, an ugly toad, whom no man had ever hunted, had been listening to the beast bragging.

"'Men kill the elephant to make boxes and jewellery from the ivory of his tusks,' he said. 'They hunt the lion and decorate their walls with his skin because his courage leads him to prey on their herds. Because he can find his way into the farmyard, the fox's fur is used on the collar of a robe. The peacock's glorious blue gold feathers are used to make a fan for a lady. It is what you boast of that is indeed your downfall.'"[34]

Review questions

1. What lesson do you learn from the above animal tale?

2. Discuss an animal tale from your community which has an important moral lesson.

10. The Clever Jackals

Once upon a time, there lived a ferocious lion in a forest. It ate up every animal it could find till there were hardly any animals left. In the forest, there also lived two jackals. They knew that their lives were in danger till the lion itself was killed. But this was an onerous task, and they had to think of an intelligent trick to trap the lion.

One day, they came up with a plan. Instead of hiding, they decided to face the lion. As soon as they heard the lion roaring nearby, they stepped out to meet him. The lion was for a moment surprised to see the jackals coming towards him.

"How come you are not running so that I can pounce on you and gobble you up"

"O king, we thought we would come and express our fear about another lion which is bigger than you that is trying to rule this jungle."

"What?" said the lion.

"I will hear of no such nonsense. There is no other lion that is the king of this jungle." "Yes, there is," said the jackals. "He lives not too far away."

The lion did not believe the jackals, but the thought of another lion ruling his kingdom and sharing his food was not something he could accept.

"Where is he? I will show him who the real ruler of this jungle is," said the lion.

"Yes, but be careful, O king, because he is really ferocious!" cautioned the jackals.

"What do you mean? Take me to him immediately"

The little jackals led the lion to a deep, round well with clear water. "There he is, Your Majesty. Down there!"

The lion moved closer to the well to have a clearer view. Lo and behold, another lion looked right back at him.

On seeing that, the lion roared and showed his teeth. And the lion in the water responded instantly by showing his teeth. The lion above was annoyed and growled, shook his mane and showed his teeth fiercely. The lion below answered by growling, shaking his mane and showed his teeth, too.

The lion above lost patience. He roared and made a terrible face. But the lion in the water made just as terrible a face.

The lion above could not take any further insult. He leaped down into the well after the other lion.

In so doing, he went after his own reflection in the water! So the poor old lion splashed and struggled down in the pond, but he could not get up the steep sides of the well and drowned.

And when he was dead, the little jackals danced and sang around the well, celebrating their cleverness and triumph.[35]

Review questions

1. What lesson do you learn from the tale above?

2. How is a lion normally depicted in your culture? How is it different from, or similar to, the way the lion is portrayed in the narrative above?

11. The World is Falling Apart

Once a rabbit lay under a coconut tree. Suddenly a scary thought came to it. What would happen to it if the world would come to an end?

Right at that moment, a monkey resting on the tree threw a coconut down and it landed next to the rabbit's head. The rabbit jumped up in fright and began to run as fast as it could.

Soon, a hare saw him. "Why are you running so fast?" he asked.

"Can't you see that the world is falling apart!" the rabbit shouted.

The hare sprinted and joined him.

They had not gone too far when an antelope saw them. "Why are you running?" asked the antelope?"

"Can't you see?" said the hare, "the world is falling apart."

The antelope turned around and joined them. One by one, they were soon joined by a giraffe, zebra, fox, deer and an elephant. They kept running without looking behind.

"Why are you all running?" asked the lion. They recognised the voice of the king of the jungle and stopped.

"O, your Majesty " they said, "the world is falling apart!"

"Who saw it falling apart?" asked the lion.

"I didn't," said the elephant. "Ask the deer."

"I didn't," said the deer. "Ask the fox."

"I didn't," said the fox. "Ask the zebra."

"I didn't," said the zebra. "Ask the giraffe."

"I didn't," said the giraffe. "Ask the antelope."

"I didn't," said the antelope. "Ask this hare."

"I didn't," said the hare. "Ask this rabbit."

At last, the lion asked the rabbit that had claimed the earth was falling apart.

"Yes, it is true, Your Majesty. I was sleeping under a tree and the earth started breaking up right next to my head!" the rabbit said.

"Show me exactly where it happened" said the lion.

The rabbit eagerly took the lion and the rest of the animals to the tree. Everything seemed in order except a coconut that lay at the spot where the rabbit had been resting.

"It must be the sound of the coconut falling on the ground that made you think the earth was falling apart. You foolish rabbit!" The lion roared and shook its mane with disgust. The animals dispersed with their heads down and the rabbit dived into a nearby burrow in shame.[36]

Review questions

1. Discuss the lesson learned from the above narrative.

2. How is the role of the lion in the above story different from the one in the previous story?

3. Narrate a story from your community that focuses on animals. Describe the human characteristics the animals represent. What is the moral of the story?

12. The Monkey and the Hotchpotch

There was once a fisherman who owned a monkey and a goat. Every morning before going fishing, he would tie the two animals around their necks and tether them to a coconut tree at the seashore. He would then cook a meal of hotchpotch made from lentils and rice in a pan, cover the food carefully and take his boat out to the sea to fish.

Every evening, when he returned, he found the pan of hotchpotch empty, and the mouth of the goat smeared with some of the food. This annoyed the fisherman a great deal. Each time, he whipped the goat for eating up his food and tied the rope more securely around its neck. But the goat never seemed to learn its lesson.

The fisherman often wondered how the goat managed to untie itself and eat the food. One day, he decided to find out. He cooked the food and hid himself behind a tree to observe what would follow.

As soon as he was out of sight, the monkey untied the rope from its neck and went straight for the pan of food. It greedily ate up all the food and then scraped off the last bits of hotchpotch from the pan and then smeared the goat's mouth with it. As it did this, it cried in amusement, "Quick, quick. You will get your dessert later."

The fisherman was shocked to see this and came out of his hiding place.

The monkey wondered why the fisherman had returned so early. However, having cleverly cleaned the pot and its mouth, the monkey was confident that the fisherman had no reason to suspect him. The fisherman got his whip out and walked over to the goat. To the monkey's amazement, the fisherman — instead of whipping the goat — patted him and asked for its apology. The fisherman then turned to the monkey and cracked his whip. "So you have been cheating me all this time, and I have been blaming the poor goat for your deeds!"

The monkey got a thorough lashing. From that day, the fisherman tied the monkey around its stomach ensuring that the knot lay on its back so that it could never unfasten itself again. [37]

Review questions

1. In about 60 words, summarise the story above.
2. Compare the character of the goat with that of the monkey.
3. Is there a way the fisherman could have saved his food so that the monkey could not get it in the first place?
4. Narrate a trickster story from your community. What is the moral of the story?

13. How the Monkey Got a Red Bottom

There was once a woman who lived in a village in Gujerat with her son. In their compound, there were lots of guava, banana, mango and paw paw trees.

Among these trees lived a monkey. The monkey ate away all the fruits that grew on the trees. It also ate all the food that the woman cooked and sometimes left unguarded in the compound.

Mother and son got fed up with the monkey and resolved to punish it. One day, they decided to invite the monkey for lunch. The monkey was quite surprised. They convinced the monkey to come by saying that it had been their neighbour for so long that they felt bad about not inviting it to their house. The monkey was quite touched by this explanation and accepted the invitation.

As the lunch was being prepared, the monkey peeped through the leaves and smelled the good food. The monkey joined the family at table when the food was finally ready. The woman and her son showed their hospitality by inviting the monkey to sit on a special red seat. This, in fact, was an iron pan which they had heated until it was redhot. The monkey, in his greed for food, was quick to sit on the hot pan.

"Quick, quick," the monkey cried as soon as it sat down. It swiftly jumped and ran away, never to be seen again. Its bottom was badly burnt. That is how the monkey got a red bottom. [38]

Review questions

1. Why were mother and son upset with the monkey?

2. What did they decide to do to punish the monkey?

3. Compare the character of the monkey in this story to the one in the previous story.

4. Compare the methods of punishment used in the two stories. Do you think the choice of punishment in each story was fair? Why or why not?

5. Narrate any other story that focuses on animals. What is the moral of the story?

Tales of destiny

There is a general belief in Indian tradition that whatever is destined to happen will happen. This is often related in the Gujerati saying: "*Je tara lekh maan likhayelu hasee teh thasee*", meaning, "Whatever is written in your fortune, that only will happen." In fact, when children are born, especially in Hindu families, some parents have their fortunes told by special fortune readers. To a great extent, Indians of nearly all religions share this belief in destiny, sometimes also termed as *naseeb*. The saying, *Karam bausao adhe adh* encourages people to adopt a more balanced view because it says that fate and personal struggle shape destiny equally. We must not solely depend on fortune for our success, because all our actions owe half their success to self-help. Self-help and confidence in our good fortune must go hand in hand. Both are equally powerful in shaping destiny. The story, 'Struggle Versus Fate' questions which between the two forces plays a bigger role. The story that follows it focuses on how one can change the course of one's destiny.

14. Struggle Versus Fate

Once, there were two friends who had an argument. One insisted that struggle was what determined success, but the other argued that it did not matter whether you struggled or not, for eventually, what mattered was written in your destiny.

If you were destined to be poor, you would remain poor despite your struggle. They both agreed to test their views.

First, the man who believed in struggle went to a poor man's hut and gave him some money to start a business. He said that he would return after six months to see how he was doing.

The poor man set aside some money for food and tied the rest carefully in his turban. He went to the big wholesale market to figure out his trade. At the end of a hard day, he was able to make a deal with a successful merchant who was willing to sell him spices cheaply. The poor old man would sell these at another market and make his profit. They decided to conclude their transactions the next day when the old man had bought his wheelbarrow to carry the spices. On his way home, the old man, who was quite hungry, bought some sweetmeats and put them on his head. Soon, a hawk flying low spotted the food and, in one swoop, picked up the sweetmeat together with the turban. The poor man lost all the money and returned home hungry.

After six months, the two friends returned to check on the old man and found that he was as poor as they had left him.

The man who believed in struggle again gave the poor man some more money and asked him to pursue his business, reminding him that he would return after six months. This time, the old man thought he would be wiser. The merchant who had initially agreed to sell spices no longer wanted to deal with the old man. Before he set out to the market to make new trade contacts, the old man hid the money in an old pot filled with sawdust. "Nobody will spot the money here," he thought to himself and left his home.

Later that day, someone knocked at the door and asked for some sawdust. The poor man's wife, kind as she was, thought for a moment and remembered the pot filled with dust. The stranger at the door did not bring a container to put the sawdust in, and so the woman gave away the clay pot. "After all," she thought, "this is old and useless to us."

When the old man returned in the evening, the first thing he did was to go and check on his money. The clay pot was nowhere to be seen. He asked his wife, who told him what she had done. The old man cried out in grief, "Alas! it is not my fate to get rich."

Six months later, the two friends returned and found the poor man in no better position than they had left him.

Now the man, who believed in fate decided to test his views. He gave the same poor man a piece of iron and said that it may be of help some day and said he would return in six months. The poor man carelessly threw the piece of iron in a corner of his house. After a couple of weeks, their neighbour, who was a fisherman, asked them for a piece of iron to tie it to his fishing net in order to weigh it down. They gladly gave away the iron which they thought would never be of any use to them.

That evening, the neighbour returned and brought them a fish as a show of gratitude for their help.

When the poor man cut open the fish, he found some real pearls in its stomach. However, the poor man had never seen anything so precious and therefore did not know that these were, in fact, real pearls. The stones were interesting enough, and so he kept them in the corner of the house. At night the pearls glistened in the darkness. The old man and wife felt that these must be some precious stones.

The next day, the poor man took the stones to a few jewellers in the town and found that each was ready to pay a very high price for them. The old man instead decided to go to the king's palace. The king saw the pearls and was taken in by the glister. He had never seen such beautiful pearls before. He gave the poor man a very large amount of money with which several generations of his family could lead a very comfortable life. When the two friends found out what had happened, they agreed that in life, fate played a greater role than struggle. [39]

Review questions

1. Do you agree with the view that fate plays a bigger role in life than struggle? Discuss.

2. Narrate a story in which either fate or struggle plays a prominent role.

15. An Offering

There was a young man by the name of Zaffar. He once went to a religious man who was known to read people's fortunes. The prophecies given by this religious man always turned out to be true. He predicted that Zaffar would die on the night of his wedding. Zaffar therefore never married, partly because of his own fear of death and partly because no parents wanted to give away their daughter because she would become a widow on the first day of marriage.

Zaffar was getting old and his mother was keen to see him settle down. Perhaps, she thought, the old man's words were after all unnecessarily scaring her son. Eventually, Zaffar agreed with her.

In the neighbourhood, there lived a girl called Fatima. She was an orphan who lived with her ageing uncle. Her uncle was very sick and was in a hurry to marry Fatima off with a hope that she would have a home after his death. Zaffar got to know about Fatima and decided to ask for her hand in marriage. Her uncle agreed, with the hope that the religious man would be proved wrong this time.

The day of the wedding was, in many ways, the happiest and the saddest day for Zaffar and Fatima. After the wedding ceremony, the bride and the bridegroom retired to their marriage quarters. Soon, there was a knock at the door. Zaffar opened the door and there stood a poor man. He asked Zaffar for food. There was no food left since the wedding guests had finished it all. Zaffar left the house and his new bride and went to the city to look for food. By the time he got the food and fed the poor man, it was dawn.

He returned to the room. Outside the room stood the religious man. Zaffar realised that it was the day after his wedding and he was still alive. The man told Zaffar that his good deed had saved him from death. The offering he made to the poor had earned him his life. Zaffar was very happy.

He and Fatima lived happily ever after. [40]

Review questions

1. What lesson do you learn from the above story?

2. Narrate a story in which things change for the better in somebody's life. Explain the reasons for the change and whether struggle or fate had a role to play.

Moral tales

Moral tales are aimed at teaching children the values of a community. Some of these values may include honesty, self-dignity, contentment, humility and sacrifice, hard work, social tolerance and humanity.

In the Indian oral tradition, many of these values are embodied in animal characters, as is demonstrated in 'The Monkey and the Crocodile' and 'The Mouse With Seven Tails'. When a story involves human characters, as in 'A Kingly Gesture' and 'Digging for Wealth', the focus is not directly on the characters, to avoid insult, but more on their actions, through the use of symbolism.

16. The Monkey and the Crocodile

There was once a monkey that lived on a big berry tree on the bank of a river. The tree bore sweet berries which the monkey ate every day. In the river lived a crocodile.

Across the river, though was another berry tree with much bigger and juicier berries. The monkey eyed the tree each day, wishing it could cross the river and eat all that sweet fruit. But alas, it could not swim.

One day, it expressed its wish to the crocodile, which was lazing around on the river bank. The crocodile raised its sleepy head and stirred its tail, "Oh if you wish to go across, I can take you!"

"How?" asked the monkey.

"Easy. On my big strong back," said the crocodile. The monkey could not pass up the offer since the thought of the sweet fruits across the river made its mouth water.

Soon, the monkey hopped onto the crocodile's back and off they went. Half-way across the river, the crocodile slowed down and then for a moment remained still.

"What is wrong?" asked the monkey.

"Oh, nothing. I just thought that since you eat those sweet berries each day, you must have a very sweet heart. And I would like to taste it!"

The monkey was shocked and scared. There was no way he could escape. He had to think fast.

43

"O crocodile, my friend, you were so kind to bring me so far across the river. I wish, however, that you would have let your wish be known earlier."

"Why?" asked the crocodile.

"You see, I do not carry my heart with me. I normally leave it up on the tree. However, I will be happy to let you have my heart if you take me back to the tree," persuaded the monkey.

"You mean we go again to the other side of the bank?"

"Yes," said the monkey. The crocodile was upset but the thought of the sweet heart made its mouth water. He turned around and swam fast to take the monkey back to its original tree. No sooner had they reached the bank, than the monkey hopped off and hastily climbed up the tree.

The crocodile waited for a long while and then lifted its head "Why are you taking so long monkey? Where is your heart?" he inquired.

The monkey took some berries from the tree and started throwing them at the crocodile, "Quik, quik, quik, Here is my heart. There is my heart! You think I am a fool to give you my heart!"

From that day, the monkey decided to remain content with the fruit from his tree and not wish for those he could not reach.[41]

Review questions

1. What lesson do you learn from the story above?

2. Describe the characterisitics of the crocodile. Can you think of another similar story?

3. Narrate a story on contentment.

17. A Kingly Gesture

A long time ago in India, there lived a maharajah or a great king. He was a good king, and people were happy in his kingdom. One day, five big boats from Persia carrying two hundred people landed on the shore of the maharajah's kingdom. The people in the boat were tired and hungry after the long journey.

They did not like the cruel king in Persia. They had, therefore, escaped and hoped for protection in the maharajah's kingdom. The leader of the Persian travellers was a high priest. The priest asked his people to stay in the boats while he went to meet the maharajah to seek permission for them to stay.

The priest reached the king's palace and was finally brought to his court. He knelt before the king and said, "O maharajah, I come here with nothing but praises for your kind and just rule. I have escaped tyranny in Persia and have come with two hundred of my people and wish to stay in your kingdom."

The king got worried. He looked at the old strange-looking priest. The ways of the people from Persia were different from the ways of his own people in India. They dressed, ate and looked different. They also sounded different! How could his people live with the Persians?

The maharajah could not say no, for this would be considered very impolite. So he ordered one of his courtiers to bring him an empty glass and a pitcher of milk. Everyone in the court watched attentively to see what the king was about to do.

The maharajah filled the glass with milk right to the brim. He carefully looked at the glass and added a few more drops of milk, ensuring it reached the brim. Satisfied that there was no more space in the glass, he carefully handed the glass of milk to the Persian priest. The clever priest understood what the king meant. The maharajah's kingdom was full. There was no more room in the kingdom for the newly arrived immigrants. The priest thought for a while, and then he requested a few grains of sugar. Raising the glass, he carefully poured the sugar into the milk. The milk did not spill, but instead turned sweet.

The king and the courtiers, on witnessing the priest's response, were very touched. The Persians were going to be like grains of sugar. Instead of displacing the Indian people, they would sweeten and enrich their lives.

The maharajah granted them permission to stay in his kingdom. [42]

Review questions

1. Describe how the priest convinced the maharajah to let his people stay in his kingdom.

2. Relate a wisdom tale from your community.

18. Digging for Wealth

There was once a farmer who had two sons. The farmer was old and sick and he knew that he was going to die soon. One evening, he called both his sons and told them about the fortune he was going to leave for them.

He said that he had hidden all his wealth in the vast fields, which he owned. He advised them to dig the land to get to the riches.

The older son, in greed, immediately started digging up the land.

He dug up half of the land and found no wealth. He became impatient and began suspecting what his father had told them to be untrue. He finally decided to go to the city to look for a job and earn his living there.

The younger son did not give up. He decided to remain on the land. He woke up early each morning and worked on the land. Once the land was dug, he planted various crops on it.

Soon the rain came and the crops flourished. The younger son prospered as a farmer. He had, indeed, found the wealth that his father had hidden in the land. [43]

Review questions

1. Compare the ways in which the two interpreted their father's will.

2. Narrate a story from your family or community which focuses on a parent or an elder giving advice. Describe the purpose and meaning of the advice.

19. The Mouse with Seven Tails

There was once a baby mouse that was born with seven tails. Whenever he went out to play, the children in the neighborhood teased him by singing:

> The mouse with seven tails.
> The mouse with seven tails.

The mouse hated this. He went home crying and complained to his mother. The mother advised the baby mouse to go to the barber and get one of the tails cut off. The baby mouse did as his mother told him.

The following day, when the mouse went out to play, the children started teasing him:

> The mouse with six tails.
> The mouse with six tails.

The baby mouse was very upset to learn that it did not help to cut one of his tails. His mother advised him to get one more of his tails chopped off at the barber's. The baby mouse did exactly that.

The next morning, the children teased him once again:

> The mouse with five tails.
> The mouse with five tails.

This went on till the baby mouse was left with just one tail. This time, he thought that this had finally solved his problem since he looked like all the other mice. But the children did not leave the baby mouse alone. They continued teasing him:

The mouse with one tail.
The mouse with one tail.

The baby mouse got fed up and decided to get rid of his last tail. The barber was surprised and asked the mouse if he really wanted him to cut off his only tail. The mouse had no doubts. The tails had after all brought him great shame.

The barber reluctantly chopped off the last tail. The mouse now thought the children had nothing to tease him about. When he went out to play the following morning, the children had yet another song to tease the mouse:

The mouse with no tail.
The mouse with no tail.

"Alas!" thought the baby mouse. "They will tease me no matter what! I wish I had remained as I was". [44]

Review questions

1. What moral lesson do you learn from this story?

2. Who do you think was most responsible for making the young mouse cut his tails? Give reasons for your answer.

3. Narrate an event where either you or someone else had to deal with a similar situation as the young mouse.

Stories of wisdom and wit

Akbar, the greatest Mogul emperor of India, was also a great statesman. The basis of his empire lay neither in religion nor in caste nor race. Akbar received the willing support of the people not only because of his policy of religious tolerance but also because he granted them freedom of social life.

Emperor Akbar was fair and just and had gathered in his court highly talented men from different religions and castes. Among these, were nine men who are renowned in history. They were called the nine gems of Akbar's court.

Birbal, Tansen, Abul Fazl and Man Singh were among these men. Birbal rose to a very high position in the court not only because of his bravery and valour, but also because of his rare wit, wisdom and humorous nature. He became a very close friend, trusted minister and associate of Emperor Akbar. Because of his enviable position in the court and his unique nature, many stories are told about him.[45] Some of these stories from India have been passed on from one generation to another in East Africa. A few examples of these are given below.

20. Counting Bangles

The courtiers in Akbar's court were jealous of Birbal because they thought that he received more attention from the emperor than they did. So out of jealousy they decided to embarrass Birbal one day. They requested Emperor Akbar to challenge Birbal by asking him a question whose answer they were sure he would not know. Since the emperor loved games of wit, he readily agreed.

When Birbal showed up in the court, Akbar asked, "Birbal, since you see your wife everyday, how many bangles does she wear on her hands altogether?"

The courtiers waited in great anticipation. They figured that if Birbal told the exact number then he would be embarrassed because they could say that he had nothing better to do than count his wife's bangles every day. And if he could not answer, then he would be embarrassed because he was so unobservant that in spite of seeing his wife's hands every day, he still could not remember how many bangles she wore.

Birbal immediately guessed the trick. He said to the emperor, "Your Majesty, if you spare my life I will answer this question."

The emperor laughed and said, "I grant you your life. Go ahead." Then Birbal said, "Your Majesty, she has the same number of bangles as one eighth the amount of hair in your beard. And since you touch your beard every day, you must already know the answer."

The courtiers were once again amazed at Birbal's wit. The emperor was so amused by this clever answer that he rewarded Birbal handsomely.

1. What do you find so witty about Birbal's replies to the emperor?

2. Narrate a tale from your community which focuses on wit.

21. The Blind and the Sighted

Matching wits with Birbal was one of the favourite pastimes of Emperor Akbar's. One day Akbar complained to Birbal, "Many of my courtiers do not do exactly what I ask them to. They behave as if they were deaf."

Birbal said, "Yes, Your Majesty. You are right. Furthermore, most of them are also blind."

"What!" said Akbar, "That is ridiculous. You know very well that they are not blind."

Birbal replied, "Your Majesty, I will prove it to you that they are so."

The next day, Birbal arrived bright and early to the court with his assistant. In the courtyard, he started digging a hole. Soon the courtiers arrived. Whoever asked him, "What are you doing Birbal?" he asked his assistant to write that person's name on a list. One by one, they came and most of them asked him the same question. Soon the emperor himself arrived and asked, "What are you doing Birbal?" Birbal asked his assistant to write the emperor's name on the list as well. The emperor asked with annoyance what the list was for. Birbal quickly replied. "This is the list of blind people in this court."

Akbar was astonished and said, "What do you mean. I am not blind." Birbal replied, "But Your Majesty, you saw what I was doing, yet you still asked me what I was doing." The emperor was delighted with Birbal's answer.

Review questions

1. Why did Birbal put down the emperor's name on the list of the blind people?

2. Narrate a similar type of story that you know of from your community or from another community.

22. The Cleverest Merchants

Once Emperor Akbar asked Birbal, "Who are the cleverest people in this land?"

Birbal thought for a while and replied, "Your Majesty, the cleverest people are the merchants."

Emperor Akbar was surprised at Birbal's reply. "How do you know? What proof do you have?"

At once Birbal asked a servant to bring a type of grain called *Moong Dal* and called for a group of leading merchants to assemble at the court.

The merchants were worried about being summoned to the royal court. After all they had committed no crime. On their arrival, Birbal distributed some grain into each of the merchant's hands. "Can you tell me what is the name of this grain?"

The Merchants were now truly concerned. They could not believe that they were being asked to identify and name the grain that was most commonly found. Each thought that there must be some trick behind this question. They stared at the grain without saying anything.

Soon, one of the chief merchants said, " Your Majesty, we wish to discuss amongst ourselves and give you the answer."

They gathered and shared their concern about being asked the name of such a common grain. There surely must be some trick to this. If they gave the obvious answer, *Moong Dal*, then the emperor may get displeased and punish them. They could not decide what to identify it as.

Birbal, after having waited for some time, asked, "how come you are taking so long. What is the name of this grain?" One of the merchants carefully said, "I think it is *Chana Dal?*"

The other said, "It looks smaller than the *Udad Dal,* but I do not remember the name of this grain."

The next one said, " I think it looks more like the *Tuvar Dal,* but I am not sure." Each merchant avoided giving the name of the grain. The emperor lost his patience, "You mean to say, that you cannot identify the *Moong Dal!*" They all immediately responded, "Yes, that is it! That is its name."

Birbal could not let them get away that easily. He understood their cleverness. Birbal insisted, "So what is its name?" One merchant said, "It is what the emperor just said."

The next one added, "Yes, it is what the emperor said a little while ago."

The third one said, "True. What the emperor said is the name of the grain, though I do not remember what his Majesty just said." The Emperor lost His patience and could not keep quiet any longer. "You mean to say you cannot remember that I just said, *Moong dal!*"

"Yes, yes that is the name," they replied together.

Soon the merchants were asked to leave the court. Birbal had proved his point. The emperor was impressed by the cleverness of the merchants.[46]

Review Questions

1. Describe the cleverness demonstrated by the merchants in the above story.

2. Narrate a story that focuses on the cleverness of a person or a group of people.

23. The True Owner of the Bag of Coins

An oil merchant went to buy some groceries one day. When he was done, he hurried back to his home and forgot his bag of coins at the grocer's shop. On realising this, he rushed back to get it.

The grocer claimed that in fact the bag was his and refused to give it back to the oil merchant. One thing led to another and they began to quarrel. Soon the quarrel became very heated. The onlookers suggested that they take their dispute to Birbal.

When Birbal heard their story, he ordered them to tell the truth. Even then, each insisted that he owned the bag of coins. There seemed to be no way out.

Birbal got an idea. He asked an attendant to bring a pan full of very hot water. He emptied the bag of coins into the pan. It did not take long before the oil from the coins floated on top. Now Birbal knew who the money belonged to.

He asked the grocer to return the bag of coins to the oil merchant immediately and imposed punishment on the grocer for lying.[47]

Review questions

1. The story above focuses on Birbal's special way of finding out to which person the bag of coins belonged. Can you figure out another way of determining the true owner of the money?

2. Narrate a story from your community in which a thief may have been caught using a clever method.

Chapter Four

RIDDLES

Riddles are witty questions often imbued with wisdom. They encompass creative and playful manipulation of words. They require two parties, one to pose the question and the other to respond.

The main purpose of posing a riddle is to outwit the respondent. In the Indian oral tradition, the riddle is often posed with linguistic or contextual ambiguity in order to confuse the respondent and create difficulty in solving the problem. The ambiguity may be brought about by using a confusing word or a phrase or one whose meaning varies depending on the way it is pronounced, or by stating a paradoxical situation. Consider the example below:

Kem bane kepaani upar pathar tare?
How does it happen that above the water float stones?

The way the question is posed makes it difficult for the respondent to explain how the stones can float above the water. The play is on the word *"tare"*, which can either mean "float" or "below" depending on how it is pronounced. The respondent who catches on to this variation in pronunciation would have the correct explanation — that the word *"tare"* means "below" and the situation is not unusual at all.

Sometimes, the linguistic ambiguity is also enhanced by a clever arrangement of words, for example:

Raja rani beh, Ladwa tren, khase kem?
The king and queen are two, the *ladwa* (sweets) are three. How will they eat (equal amounts without breaking any of the *ladwa*)?

The respondent will think of the king and queen as a pair, adding up to two people because the plural of the noun *rani* (queen) is the same as the singular. The respondent will, therefore, probably get confused about the distribution of three *ladwa* between the two. On the other hand, the challenger is actually saying that there is one king and two queens and, therefore, the number of people actually adds up to three. Since there are three *ladwa*, they can, therefore, be equally divided.

The contextual ambiguity is sometimes created by presenting a riddle about a plant, fruit or an inanimate object by comparing it to a living creature to confuse the respondent.

Hun chun lambo taar, mari chamri no rang leelo, maru lohi sawaad, maaro maas haraam. Hun kon?
I am tall, my skin is green, my blood is sweet, and my flesh is forbidden. Who am I?

The riddle sets the respondent to think in the context of a creature with animal characteristics. However, the answer to the riddle is "sugar cane", which also has the attributes described in the riddle.

Riddles have played an important role in Asian culture. In certain communities in India, girls used riddles to test the intellectual prowess of young men who came as suitors. Chieftains used to compete in riddling, as they did in boxing and wrestling, sometimes staking their lives on the outcome.

Historically, riddles were part of the culture of the royal courts. There is a Punjabi legend about King Sirikap who entertained riddles from visitors and if the king could not answer, he would reward the visitor with a white chariot. As the legend goes, one day Raja Sirikap was visited by a royal guest, King Rasalu, who asked a complex double riddle:

"Within your city boundary,
A wonder I did note:
A horse and sixty villages
Were swallowed by a goat.

Then came a bald-headed urchin, most capacious maw,
Who stooped him down and guzzled up
The Ravi and Chenab." [48]

The riddle as reported described two things which King Rasalu had witnessed on the way to the King Sirkap's palace. First, he noticed a retired old soldier washing clothes on a river bank. On the drier ground the soldier had left under his turban an important paper granting him a reward of a horse and an income from 60 villages. As the soldier washed clothes, a goat came and ate up the paper. Next, as he walked further, Rasalu saw two boys playing. Each boy had made a small pool of water and while one claimed it to be River Ravi the other claimed his pool was River Chenab. Just then, a bald-headed boy appeared, stooped down and drank up all the water from the two pools.

King Sirikap could not solve the riddle, and he gave a white chariot to King Rasalu. [49]

Riddling was also an integral part of the culture of the royal courts during the Mogul rule in India. As earlier mentioned, Emperor Akbar had collected able men from different religions and castes in his court. They were the so-called Nine Gems of Akbar's court. Among these, Birbal rose to a very high position because of his wit and wisdom in solving problems.

The Emperor once entered the court and asked all his wise men, "Do you know where the seed of a tree is located?" All the courtiers thought for a long time, but could not give him an acceptable answer. The emperor sent for Birbal.

When Birbal entered the court, he was asked, "Where is the seed of the tree located?"

Birbal immediately asked a servant to bring him some water. When the water was brought, Birbal sprinkled some here and there on the ground and said, "There is a seed at this place and at that place."

The Emperor and the courtiers were astonished. When asked the meaning of this, Birbal replied, "Your Majesty, the seeds of trees are situated everywhere in the earth itself. They only need water. As soon as some drops of water fall on the earth, these seeds grow. So, one can regard that wherever water falls, seeds are certain to be there!" [50]

The emperor, delighted with Birbal's answer, rewarded him well.

On another occasion, the emperor asked, "Birbal, what is the distance between true and false?" [51]

"Four fingers wide," Birbal replied.

The emperor could not understand. He asked, "How is it so?"

Birbal said, "Your Majesty, what we see with our own eyes is true and what we hear by our ears is false. The distance between our eyes and ears is four fingers wide."[52] Once again, Birbal had won Akbar's heart with his wit and wisdom.

To date, riddles are a favourite game for adults and children in many Asian homes, and this pastime has remained a key part of Asian culture in East Africa. At family and large gatherings, sometimes old and young wits are tested with riddles and teased with catchy questions.

Riddles collected in this chapter originate from different parts of India and are collected from the Gujerati, Cutchi, Punjabi, and Urdu-speaking communities. While there is no single way to classify the riddles, they are divided in this book into the following categories: riddles about cosmology and the physical universe; riddles about plants, fruits and vegetables; riddles about small living creatures, parts of the human body, and inanimate objects, and wisdom riddles.

The following are examples of riddles. The answers to all the riddles are given at the end of this chapter.

Riddles on natural phenomena and cosmology

1. If anyone can catch it, I will give him a thousand rupees.[53]
2. What stands up without support?[54]
3. Who will wash the jungle?[55]
4. Who will sweep the jungle?[56]
5. A smooth bed has been spread, yet nobody sleeps in it. What is it?[57]
6 One goes and never gets tired, another sits and never rises, and another stands and never sits. Who are we?
7. I can see it fall, but I cannot catch it.
8. A handful of parched rice scattered over the whole yard.
9. A basketful of fried paddy which cannot be counted.
10. A new pot with seven holes.

Riddles on plants, fruits and vegetables

In these types of riddles, the challenger normally describes a thing and the respondent has to guess the answer.

11. *Baap leelo, ma kesri ane bacha kara. Hun kon?*
    Father green, mother orange, children black. Who am I?

12. Who is the little boy with green or red clothes that can make a whole village weep?

13. Whose is that good elegant body that even handsome people eat? It is shaped like the dome of a minaret, and wears red and white clothing. Whoever kills it must weep over it.

14. The children are gods, but their mother is a devil. What is that?[58]

15. "Oh, father, I fell down! Oh, mother, I fell down! And as soon as I fell down, a calf ate me."

16. There is something to eat, something to drink, something to chew on, something for the cow to eat, and something to sow in the garden! Yet there is only one thing.

17. There is something with three eyes in the forehead and with feathers spread like a peacock's.

18. What is a cowshed full of cows with all their horns pointing down?[59]

19. I have a green turban and black robe. What am I?

20. We throw away the flesh and eat the bones. What is this?

21. During my early years, I wear a *saree* (long wrap dress) of green colour. In my youth, a crest grows upon my head; and then, my beard and moustache also grow. When I get old, I wear pendant ornaments studded with diamonds and pearls. Who am I?

22. I planted flowering shrubs in knee-deep water. When the water was reduced to a very low level, the flowers bloomed.

23. A green house and a red mother with black children. Who am I?

24. A small ball containing 50 to 100 grains.

25. First, my mother and I were born, then father. For five days nothing happened, then my grandfather was born.

Riddles on living creatures

26. What animal can swallow its own head?[60]

27. It lives in the water and is not a fish; it wags two horns and is not a buffalo. What is it?

28. What is that which is red in colour, has six legs, and moves about even when its stomach is cut?

29. Cattle of the same shed. When collected (all) are white, when broken some will be black, some will be white and some will be red.

Riddles on parts of the human body

30. There are two brothers, born in the same house, having the same name, exercising great power of life, yet they have no power of life in themselves.

31. On one chair sit five brothers. Although touching, they do not touch one another.

32. Below the thicket is glistening; below the glistening a foaming; below the foaming a chattering. What is that? [61]

33. While the king's son sits eating rice, his two sons stare at him. What is that?

34. Five brothers are entering a jagged hollow at the same time.

Riddles on inanimate objects

35. What golden parrot drinks with its tail? [62]

36. Two fingers seize me and carry me to two caves. What is that? [63]

37. A place where there is a village without people, and where there is a river without water. Where is that?

38. What runs fast with a thousand people in it? [64]

39. It is white but is not sugar, it is bright but is not glass, it melts but is not snow, and you eat it every day. What is it? [65]

40. What is that shining beauty with whom everybody is in love? Whoever is lucky enough to win her can have everything he wants.

41. What runs into the earth in the morning and doesn't come out again until noon? [66]

42. What is that thing which is held by five and used for the adornment of 32.

43. "Come along, you five brothers! Push me past the white stones." Who is speaking?

44. Who stands dumb until he is slapped, then he speaks out?

45. Silver branches stretched across a ceiling. Wise said to Witty, "Who tied them?" What is that?[67]

46. Black crows sit on a white bank and say, "Caw, caw!" What is that?[68]

47. It fruits not and flowers not, nor do its branches bend down; and as long as one lives, one eats it.

48. It is your hand, but you cannot catch it. What is it?

49. When it stands still, it is of no value. When it moves, it imparts coolness. It is useless during the winter and offers pleasure during the summer. What is that?

50. Without arms, without legs, carried on the shoulder. Murder is in its mouth, and it eats men as they stand. What is it?

51. A baby in an open field with a basin of fire on his head being kissed while his stomach gurgles. Who is that?

52. A big container of water cannot be lifted. Help me to lift it, oh my God! What is it?

53. What is it that has two heads and moves without feet?

54. What is it that walks and runs during the day and rests not alone at night?

55. What is it that keeps awake during the night and sleeps during the daytime?

56. What goes up to the river and then stops?

57. What a stunted little thing! And it has a plait of hair a yard long?[69]

58. A man is lazy. He walks sitting down. How is that?

59. When put down it is silent, when picked up it is noisy. What is it?

60. What is the thing which stays in the ground and turns into bars of gold the next morning?

61. I dropped it into water and it arose like a king parrot. What is that?

62. A populated village goes over the water. What is that?

63. A person who is speechless while alive but speaks fluently when he is dead. He has no skin on his body after death, yet takes part in ceremonies. What is that?[70]

Wisdom riddles

These riddles pose a problem which requires knowledge, wisdom and a logical solution.

64. **Two fathers and two sons.**

    Two fathers and two sons went fishing. Each had one fish, though they caught only three fish. How can this be?

65. **Crossing the river**

    Once there was a man with a lion, a goat and some grass. The man needed to cross the river. His boat was too small and could hold only him and one other thing. How could he carry the lion, goat, and grass so that the lion would not eat the goat and the goat would not eat the grass?

66. **Two mothers**

    Once two women came to a wise man, each claiming that a little boy was her son. The wise man asked the women to stand on each side of the boy and pull his hand. Whoever was stronger and was able to pull the boy over to her side could claim the boy. The women did what the wise man suggested and began pulling the boy's hand. Soon, the boy began to cry in pain. One of the women stopped pulling and said the other woman was stronger and could therefore have the boy. The wise man, in fact, gave the boy to the woman who had stopped pulling. Why was this so?

67. **A drink for the crow**

    Once a thirsty crow flew down and perched at the edge of a big pitcher, but saw only a little bit of water remaining at the bottom. He tried to reach it with its beak but the pitcher was too deep. But when it was about to give up it suddenly knew what to do. It flew to and from the garden to the pitcher till it was able to drink easily. What did the crow do?

68. **Sticks of truth**

    Once a rich man came to a wise man complaining that his daughter's diamond ring had been stolen. The ring disappeared while his daughter was bathing and, therefore, the rich man was sure that it was taken by one of the servants. How was he to catch the thief? The wise man asked

59

for all the servants to appear at his court. He gave each of them sticks of similar length to take home and keep under the bed during the night. He added that the stick belonging to the thief would grow two inches longer over the night.

The next day, the wise man had all the servants come and hold up their sticks. None of them had grown any longer. Then suddenly the wise man called out, "This is the thief. His stick is two inches shorter!"

Once caught, the servant confessed that he had stolen the ring and returned it to the rich man's daughter. The wise man had said that the longer stick would belong to the thief; instead, it was the shortest stick. How did this happen?[71]

Solutions to riddles

1. The wind.
2. The sky.
3. The rain.
4. Wind.
5. Snow or ice on water.
6. Water, earth, and sky.
7. Shooting star.
8. Stars in the sky.
9. Constellations.
10. 7 days of a week.
11. Paw paw or papaya.
12. Chilli pepper.
13. An onion.
14. Roses on a thorny bush.
15. A leaf fallen from a tree.
16. A watermelon.
17. A coconut.
18. A bunch of bananas.
19. An eggplant.
20. Grain.
21. Maize.
22. Growing rice.
23. Watermelon.
24. A pomegranate.
25. Cotton.
26. A turtle.
27. A snail.
28. Ant.
29. Eggs and chickens.
30. Nostrils.
31. Ears, eyes and nose.
32. Hair, eyes, nose and mouth.
33. The two knees sticking up while a man sits and eats.
34. Fingers at meals.
35. An oil lamp.
36. Snuff (carried by thumb and finger to nostrils).

37. On a map.

38. A train.

39. Salt.

40. Money.

41. A plough.

42. Stick used as a toothbrush.

43. Rice (He is telling the fingers to put it into the mouth).

44. A drum.

45. A spider's web.

46. Writing on paper.

47. Salt.

48. Your shadow.

49. A fan.

50. A gun.

51. A *hookah* or a smoking pipe.

52. A well

53. A ship (two ends of a ship are considered as heads).

54. Shoes

55. A lamp.

56. Taking shoes off before entering water.

57. Needle and thread.

58. A man riding a bicycle.

59. A drum.

60. Fire.

61. A cork.

62. A ship.

63. A drum.

64. There were three people who went fishing. A boy, his father and his grandfather: two sons and two fathers.

65. He could take the goat over and go back alone. Then take the lion over and then bring the goat back. Then take the grass over and leave it with the lion and come back alone. And in the final trip, take the goat over.

66. The contest was not of strength but of love. The boy's true mother could not bear to see her son suffer and let go. She wanted him safe even though she could not have him.

67. The crow gathered pebbles and dropped them into the pitcher until the water rose to the top.

68. None of the sticks were magical. The thief was worried and cut off two inches of stick at night to hide its growth. Since the sticks were not magical, his stick ended up being the only short one.

Review questions

1. Study each of the riddles in the chapter. Select any three riddles from each section which impress you most. Discuss reasons for your selection.

2. Collect and write down at least five riddles from your community. Specify under which category you would place each of the riddles presented. You may identify a new category. Study each riddle collected and note how it aims to confuse the respondent.

Project suggestions

1. Organise a class session on riddling. Make sure that the student who poses the riddle states the community from which the riddle originated. You may also want to make a collection of these riddles and record them.

2. Invite a group of adults to your school and have them share some riddles with you.

3. Create a class book on riddles and make a copy of it for your school or local library.

Chapter Five

PROVERBS

Proverbs are a significant genre of Asian oral literature. They are used in various social contexts, both formal and informal. They use imagery and symbolism built around humans, animals and the physical world to convey culturally accepted beliefs and values.

Proverbs often communicate a deep message or an idea and reveal a people's philosophy of life. While other forms of literature, such as songs and riddles, may be used in a more organised social context, proverbs are normally delivered spontaneously or on the spur of the moment. They may be used to provide worldly wisdom on life. Proverbs are more effectively used by someone who is skilful in language and who knows when to use what words.

It is customary among Indians for older rather than younger people to use proverbs since, apart from their experience with language, their social standing puts them in a better position to advise the youth. Proverbs may be used in households or in gatherings, both small and large.

In the Asian oral tradition, proverbs are used for a variety of reasons and in various situations as described later in this chapter. They may, for example, be used to inspire certain attitudes or actions.

1. *Bandhyo maanas bhukhe mare.*
   A man who is tied (or homebound) dies hungry.

2. *Fareh teh chareh.*
   A person who roams (or travels) advances.

The two Gujerati proverbs above aim at getting people to take up challenges in the world outside of home. It is possible that such proverbs may have, to

63

some extent, inspired early Indian settlers to form certain attitudes about the virtue of travelling, thus encouraging them to leave their homelands and travel to East Africa in search of livelihoods and opportunities for advancement.

Moral and ethical values are held in high esteem in Asian communities. There are, therefore, proverbs to caution against vices such as dishonesty, greed and foolishness. The proverb given below, for example, is a lesson given to those who act out of greed to the point where their greed distorts their thinking and makes them to foolishly enter into dealings where they lose all that they have.

Lena ek, na dena du.
Neither take one nor give two.

The following short story illustrates this further.

"Once there was a peacock and a tortoise living on the banks of a stream. The peacock enjoyed displaying its colourful plumage and amusing its friend. One day, a bird-catcher caught the peacock and was about to take it to the market. The tortoise was greatly upset to see his friend taken captive and begged the bird-catcher to let him loose.

The bird-catcher would not be persuaded to free the peacock. The tortoise then promised a valuable present and dived into the stream. He came up with a large pearl. The bird-catcher, on seeing the shiny big pearl, readily let go of the peacock in exchange for the pearl.

The bird-catcher left but soon returned. The clever tortoise, in the meantime, had asked his friend to disappear in the bushes. The bird-catcher complained that the tortoise had not paid him well for freeing his friend and that the tortoise should get him another pearl to match the first one.

The tortoise was annoyed by the bird-catcher's greed and said, 'Fine, give me the first pearl, so that I can find one exactly like it.'

The greedy bird-catcher foolishly passed on the pearl, and the tortoise dived into the stream calling out, 'I am no fool to take one and give two.' With that, the tortoise disappeared, leaving the bird-catcher with nothing." [72]

Proverbs may also be used to resolve disputes, praise good deeds, advise in matters of money, and remind people about work and responsibility. Sometimes, proverbs are used to reveal both the serious and humorous side of life and also relate peculiarities and traits of characters, as the following does by pointing out absent-mindedness or lack of understanding in a person.

Sari Ramayan kay gaii, Sita koni hati?
After the whole Ramayana has been told, (he inquires) whose wife is Sita?

The above proverb is used to chide a person who sits through a whole story, play or epic or even a class discussion, and yet asks at the end a question about who the main character was. The proverb may be used to encourage a person to be more attentive.

While proverbs are used at times to soften the blow so that the message does not pain the recipient, they can also add punch to a line to clearly communicate the meaning to an opponent. The next proverb cautions someone against showing off or making a vain display.

Bahar lambi lambi dhoti, gharma masur ne roti.
When out he wears a long fancy *dhoti*, at home he eats *masur* and bread.

A *dhoti* is a dress worn by men around the lower torso. Long *dhotis* are worn only by the well-to-do and fashionable. *Masur* is a type of lentil usually eaten by the poor. The proverb is used to refer to one who attempts to show off a wealth or talent they do not really have.

Sometimes, proverbs are used to reveal conditions of a people or a country. When a country is undergoing political unrest and is without justice because of its foolish ruler, the following proverb may be used.

Andher nagri kbuddhi raja, Takeh ser bhaji takeh ser khaja.
In an ill-governed country with a foolish ruler, both the spinach and the sweetmeat have the same value.

There is no distinction between *bhaji*, spinach which may grow wildly, from *khaja*, which is an expensive sweetmeat. In other words, no distinction is made between the good and the bad, the deserving and the undeserving. In such a state of confusion, merit is not recognised.

Proverbs in this chapter are drawn from various Indian communities speaking Gujerati, Marathi, Punjabi, Cutchi, Sindhi and Urdu. Although proverbs may be classified in many different ways, in this chapter they are grouped under headings that relate to power of the tongue, domestic matters.

money and wealth, and land and cultivation. There are also proverbs about friendship, about human characteristics such as arrogance and foolishness and proverbs about theft, miserliness and generosity. Included also are proverbs about education, knowledge, and wisdom. Proverbs in this chapter are given in either both the original Indian language and English translation or simply in English. Many of the proverbs given below are self-explanatory, but where necessary, further explanations are provided.

Power of the tongue

1. *Nasibwaara zabaan chalaawe ane nasibwagernah pegh chalaawe.*
   The fortunate uses his tongue and the unfortunate his legs.[73]

2. *Men bhavtu khavu nahi, ane men bhavtu bolvu nahi.*
   Do not eat all that you like nor speak all that you know.

3. *Je karwa men rahe, se tonti se bahe.*
   Whatever is in the vessel will come out of the spout. [74] (Refers to a person who cannot keep a secret).

4. The very same tongue brings us honour or shame.

5. An iguana has two tongues. Does man also have two? (A man should not be like an iguana with two tongues, a hypocrite saying one thing to the face and something else behind a person's back.)

6. The tongue is a sword; the tongue kills and the tongue saves.[75]

7. Excessive sharpness is as bluntness.

8. With a blow of the breath the lamp is lit and with a blow it is extinguished! (The same mouth is used to give words of hope or despair)

9. If your foot slips, you may recover your balance, but if your mouth slips, you cannot recover your words.

10. Time flies, words last.[76]

Domestic matters

11. *Ghar ma chokrav ganti chaate ne upathia ne ato.*
    The children in the house lick the millstone, and the visitor gets the flour. (Said of one who makes a display of things he cannot afford.)

12. *Garma antharu ane masjid ma diwo.*
    It is dark in the house, but there is a lamp in the mosque. (This proverb has a similar message to the one preceding it except that it is set in a religious context. You do not become favourable in the eyes of God by decorating the mosque before first meeting the needs of your home.)

13. All are kings in their own houses.

14. Earn as a servant and eat as a master.[77]

15. A kind reception is better than a feast.

16. *Dour thee doongar raryamna laageh.*
    Mountains look beautiful from a distance.[78] (The proverb advises people to examine something or someone more closely before making a judgment. What may appear good from a distance may not turn out to be so when studied closely. A man overwhelmed by a woman's beauty may be cautioned with this proverb.)

17. *Miyan bibi raazi, tow kya kare kazi.*
    (When both) man and woman are willing (satisfied consenting parties), what is the *kazi* (religious magistrate) to do?
    (Love defies law. When two parties are in agreement the role of the magistrate is irrelevant.)

18. Eat your dry bread and drink cold water.
    (Do not look at others' buttered bread or make your heart thirsty.)

19. *Ghar men kharchi na, deurhi par nanch.*
    He cannot afford his daily house expenses, yet puts up a dance at his gate (for show).

20. All are good housewives where there is plenty; all patches of land are good if it has rained copiously.

21. The pan is earthen when broken by the mother-in-law but golden if broken by the daughter-in-law

22. The pot broken by the mother-in-law was a cracked pot; the pot broken by the daughter-in-law was a new pot.

23. *Ek hathe tali na waage.*
You cannot clap with only one hand.[79]
(In case of conflict, make sure not to blame just one, but hear out the other side, since both parties may be responsible for the problem. Also said of any action requiring the cooperation of others, which was not given.)

24. *Paanch aangri sarkhi nathi.*
All five fingers are not equal.[80]
(This is to accept individual differences and show respect to all members of the same family or community).

25. What is given to a kinsman (or family) is never thrown away.

26. The tell-tale causes the downfall of a kingdom.
(The man who divulges home secrets [the tell-tale] brings about the ruin of a house.)

27. *Dhaku hane dhiu khe te sikhe nunh.*
If you rebuke your own daughter, it is your daughter-in-law who will learn. (You must set a good example by treating your own family well if you want someone else to do the same.)

28. If the members of your family point their fingers at you, the outsiders will point with their toes.

Money and wealth

29. *Tipe tipe sarover banthai, kankre kankre paar banthai.*
Drop by drop, the oceans are filled; stone by stone the mountains are built. (This Gujerati proverb cautions people who lack patience and want quick results. Great tasks can be achieved step by step. This proverb is often used when advising about money. A person can become rich by saving pennies.)

30. *Savar aahre pere dhirgher.* Or *Chadar dekh ke per phailao.*
Stretch your legs according to the length of the quilt.

(This Sindhi and Urdu proverb advises people to live within their means. The proverb can be taken in an economic sense. It is not wise to live beyond your means. Cut your coat according to the cloth.)

31 Money saved is money earned.

32. Where misers live, the cheats won't starve.[81]

33. Money is ours, but not we of the money.[82]

34. When money goes, it goes with wings.[83]

35. Grain, peace, and official position — these three are the foundations of wealth. Gambling, immorality, and debt — these three are the destruction of wealth.

36. Debt is a misfortune.

37. Your creditor will wish you well, your debtor will wish you ill.

38. Twenty in hand are better than 30 borrowed.

39. A sick man's food and a debtor's earnings (are similar.)

40. The offence given by not lending is to be preferred to the annoyance caused after lending.

41. *Kauri kauri kail bator; ruppya bhail tal le gail chor.*
     The miser's loss is sudden. He gathered every possible penny, but a thief stole it.

42. *Paysa haathno mel che*
     Money is like dirt on hands. It can get washed away easily. (The proverb also points to the relative unimportance of money.)

43. *Haarto jugaari bamnu raame.*
     A losing gambler risks double.

44. Remains of a debt, a sore, or of fire should not be left unattended.

Land, cultivation and work

45. Fortune comes at random, but ploughing cannot fail.[84]

46. The best occupation is farming, trade is middling, working for another is worst of all: below that comes begging from door to door.

47. Cultivating at the proper time is equal to seven ploughings.[85]

48. O cultivator! Reap thy harvest as soon as it is ripe; if thou wilt go on thinking and hesitating, birds will consume it.[86]

49. He who did not thresh quickly carried home nothing; some stalk got wet and some the wind blew away.

50. To plough wet land and sow dry land is to waste all your labour.

51. Those farmers are best who stay at home when they have done their farming work.

52. Urgent work should be done by oneself.

53. If responsible work be given to you, you acquire double strength.

Friendship

54. Broken friendship and split pearls cannot be mended.[87]

55. If iron is broken, it may be united, but if friendship is broken, it cannot be healed.

56. If you befriend an ass, expect nothing but a shower of kicks.

57. An open enemy is better than a secretive friend.

58. Enmity with a wise man is better than friendship with a fool.

59. Boiled water has no taste (broken friendship).

60. Test a friend in trouble, and a housewife when there is nothing left in the house.

61. Though the friendship of two is so close as not to admit a hair between, it will still be destroyed by money transactions between them.

62. If a friend's mother dies, a thousand people remain (because a friend is alive), but if the friend is dead, there is none left.

Foolishness

63. The fool talks, and the wise man thinks.

64. What won't a fool say, and what won't men eat in a famine?

65. He is a fool who expects anything from unripe crops or a cow in calf.

66. A fool's property is enjoyed by the cunning.

67. A fool worries himself (kills himself) with others' concerns.

Arrogance

68. He cannot afford rice-porridge, yet he drinks wine. (Extravagance in a person).

69. Bracelets on his wrists, and his stomach is burning with hunger.

70. Empty stomach (and grains of rice) on his moustache.

71. *Apanen munh miyan mitthu.*
Self-praise is no praise.

72. She cannot dance, (and says) the courtyard is crooked.[88]

73. First he is a beggar, and secondly he demands sweetmeats as alms.

74. False gold is very bright.

Thieves and misers

75. *Chor jaisne hira ke, wasine khira ke.*
A thief is a thief, whether he steals a diamond or a cucumber.[89]

76. *Chor na jane mangni ka basan.*
A thief will not stop at a borrowed plate.[90] (A thief will not hesitate to steal a plate that you have borrowed from someone else.)

77. *Chamri veeneh pan damri naa veeneh.*
To lose the skin but not a penny. (Refers to a miser who is willing to lose something very close to him, as long as he gains a penny.)

78. A hardened person has no pain, a miser no happiness.

79. A greedy man has no taste and a lazy man no rest.

80. Iron is cut by iron.
(Set a thief to catch a thief.)

Education and knowledge

81. A well-read man is like a finely cut diamond.[91]

82. The trees bend when they bear fruit.
    (Refers to the importance of modesty when one acquires education or knowledge.)

83. Like teacher like student. [92]

84. Though the stab of the sword may fail, the stab of the pen will not fail.

85. *Aatho garyo chalke gano.*
    Half-filled pot splashes (ripples) a lot. (Told to a person who does not have much knowledge or education but shows off.)

86. When a person gets stuck, wisdom comes to him.

87. The crow went to learn the ways (walk) of the goose, but lost its own.[93]
    (One who abandons his natural or traditional ways to ape those of others is very apt to lose his self-respect and make a fool of himself.)

88. He who cannot see the light itself, what can he see with light?

89. *Jyaa suraaj na pohche tya kawih pohche.*
    Where the sun cannot reach, even there a poet will reach.[94]

90. *Thor kailan Tulsidas[95] bahut kailan kabita.*
    Critics think that they have more to say than even the poet Tulsidas himself.[96]

91. *Likhe ne pare, nam Abul Fazl.*
    He neither knows how to read nor write, but styles himself as *Abul Fazl[97]*.

92. One and one are eleven.
    (Refers to the importance of working together. Two heads are better than one.)

Wisdom

93. *Pake gare kera kana pawandha.*
    Once a potter has hardened the pot, no finer edges can be added.

(Refers to the importance of raising children well while they are young otherwise it is difficult to change their character once they mature.)

94. *Karam bausao adhe adh.*
Fate and self-exertion are half-and-half. (Fate and self-help equally shape our destiny.)

95. *Dat ne aahe zaat teh jo wahe so lahe.*
Talent is not inherited.

96. By remembering our own fault, we forget another's.

97. When one spits on the moon, it falls back on oneself.
(Advises against showing contempt towards a person of higher standing for it will only expose you in a negative way.)

98. If you throw a stone into filth, the filth will fly into your face.

99. If you kick a thorn, it will surely prick you.
(Advises against getting involved with people or in situations that are dangerous and can harm you.)

100. *Baandhi muuthi lakhjeh fuuteh toh kakhjeh.*
A closed fist is worth a million and an open fist is worth ashes.
(When a person's secrets are unknown he may be respected or valued, but when he is exposed [especially of bad deeds] he is worthless.)

101. Annoyance at the beginning is better than annoyance at the end.

102. If you remove stone by stone, even a mountain will be levelled.
(If you persistently work at something, you will succeed in completing the task. This proverb may also be used to encourage one in persuading a stubborn person to agree to something.)

103. *Boleh ena bor wenchai.*
The one who speaks, his berries will be sold.
(The proverb teaches people to exert effort when they want to achieve something. It is important to be active, known, outspoken, and in some ways assertive to get your goods sold or to accomplish your task.)

104. No strength within and no respect without. [98]

105. Hold firm on all sides, and then mount your horse.
(Take care of all details and then take action.)

106. *Jevu ker tevu ver.*
As we sow, so we reap.[99]

107. *Talmathi dungar karwu.*
To make a mountain out of a sesame seed.[100]
(This proverb describes the attitude of some people who make a big issue out of a small and insignificant thing.)

108. *Ek naa ne soh sukh.*
One refusal kills a hundred miseries.

109. *Jehne mun jitu tehne dunya jiti.*
One that conquered his passions conquered the whole world.

110. If you are good, the world is good.

111. *Jevo des tevo wes.*
As is the country, so is the dress.

112. A harvest of peace is produced from a seed of contentment.

113. He who dug a pit for others has got his legs into it.

114. He who has suffered can sympathise with those in pain.

115. One man is intoxicated with the juice of the grape, another with the juice of vegetables.[101]
(Pride dwells in everyone, rich and poor.)

116. A crow, another crow, a hundred crows. [102]
(A lie increases as it spreads.)

117. Life is like the flame of a lamp; it needs a little oil now and then.[103]

118. The ambitious man dies for fame, the glutton for his belly. [104]

119. The good horse needs but once to be nudged, just as the good man needs but once to be spoken to.[105]

120. Hunger knows no taste, sleep knows no comfort, lust knows no shame.

121. *Haathi na dant; jowana juda, ane khawana juda.*

The tusk and teeth of an elephant. One set for show and the other to eat with.
(Take caution against those who play double parts.)

122. *Parbas banda sukh kya jane.*
    A dependent knows no happiness.

123. *Jenwar jarela ainthan na jare.*
    The rope burns, but not the twist. (Refers to someone who always sticks to a habit no matter what.)

124. *Na ati bakta, na ati chup, na ati barkha, na ati dhup.*
    Neither too much talk nor too great a silence, neither continuous rain nor continuous sun is desirable.[106]
    (One is advised to seek a balance or a happy medium in their interactions with others.)

Review questions

1. Select at least four proverbs from each of the above sections and discuss what lessons you can learn from each and how you can apply them in your life.

2. Write and discuss ten proverbs you know that fall under any of the categories mentioned in this chapter.

3. Write down five different proverbs in your language and translate them into English. Determine in what categories they may be classified. Discuss the context in which these proverbs are used and what message each proverb conveys?

Chapter Six

SONGS

Songs continue to play an important role in Indian communities in East Africa, especially at religious and social occasions. There are songs to celebrate life and mourn death; songs for birth; cradle songs; play songs for children; songs of love and marriage; festival songs of fun and humour; farewell songs; songs of the seas and of travel; songs of seasons; *garba* and *rasa* dance songs; and songs for gods and goddesses.

The fabric of human life is interwoven with song and music. While the Hindi films keep the Asian community in East Africa up to date with the more contemporary songs from India, children and adults continue to be exposed to traditional songs locally. Some of these songs are in the form of prayer or praise for sacred beings, for example singing *bhajans* in the temple or recitals of *marsiyas* in some Muslim gatherings.

Adults and children are sometimes seen challenging each other to come up with songs beginning with a certain letter or sound. Normally such games begin with a somewhat meaningless verse such as:

Antakadi, bantakadi,
jena maathe
bhith padi.

Since the last word *padi* ends with the *"di"* the opponent is expected to begin a song with that sound. The opponent then challenges the other party to begin a song starting with the ending of their song. The party that cannot come up with any more songs from the cue given by the opponent loses the game.

While many of the songs sung for and by children are gradually getting lost over generations in East Africa, some have been captured in this chapter.

The lullaby and the play songs cited are among those one of the authors grew up with as a child.

Lullabies

Lori Lori Lakhani

Lori lori lakhani
Kachi keri kakani
Paki bor mamani
Ful pacheri bhaini.

Lullaby Lullaby A Hundred Thousand

Lullaby lullaby a hundred thousand
Raw mangoes for paternal uncle
Ripe berries for maternal uncle
Flowered scarf for brother.

The above lullaby identifies for the child the various members of the family, placing value on family relations. Young children playing a hand-game sing the play song below. The song has no specific meaning.

Ilu pilu chandera,
Baine mohre mutera,
Kon jaane adu padu,
Sairi sakar, khajuri no tipo

Children sit on the floor in a circle with their hands placed palm down in front of them. One child sings the song and points at every hand in the circle. Where the song ends, the child pointed at may change the position of his or her hand into a fist. The game continues with the song being repeated and the previous hand movement imitated. The game ends with all children placing their hands on each other and singing the play song together.

During the rainy season, one of the songs sung is *Avaryo warsaad.*

Avaryo warsaad

Avaryo warsaad
Gheverio prashad
Uni uni rotli aney karela nu saag

The Rain Pours

The rain pours
Sweet food offerings
Hot chapatti and bitter vegetable curry.

The above song emphasises not only the sweet food offerings that children enjoy but also the importance of *karela,* a bitter vegetable that is known to have medicinal value to keep some sicknesses away during the rainy season.

Following are some other examples of songs covering some aspects of human life. [107]

Children's songs

Traditionally, it is thought that every woman craves for a child. She desires to be a mother. If, after marriage, some years pass without her getting a baby, everybody in the family, including her husband, begins to doubt her fertility. Some consider it inauspicious to see the face of a barren woman.

Women pray for children. In the following song, a woman goes to the temple of the goddess Rannadey, the wife of the sun, to worship and ask to be blessed with a child.

Craving for a child

O' Rannadey, the wife of the great Sun,
The protector of my family, I worship Thee,
Falling at Thy feet.
Accept from me these precious ornaments,
And favour me with a child, a child to play with.

O Goddess! Open the gates of Thy closed temple.

I have come to worship Thee with all my faith.
I have this *saree* nicely washed and ironed,
Bless me with one who shall trample it.
I have my courtyard nicely dunged but barren,
Bless me with one
Who shall trample the yard,
And leave *small footprints upon it.* [108]

When a woman gets a child, she is overjoyed. In the following song, the
mother is trying to put her child to bed.

Halo to Ghano Vhalo

(1)
Halo to ghano vhalo rey
Bhai taney ramava ramakadan alo
Bhai to maro daahyo rey,
Tun pataley besi nhay.

(2)
Halo to ghano vhalo rey
Paraniyun paravadun rey
Bhai tarun ghodiyun ghughariyalu,
Suvey suda ney suvey pankhi ek na suvey ben rajvansi.

The Cradle Is So Dear to My Son

(1)
The cradle is so dear to my son,
I give you toys to play with,
Sleep! My baby, sleep!
My son is so wise,
He bathes sitting on a wooden stool,
Sleep! My baby, sleep.

(2)
The cradle is so dear to my baby,
The cradle is ringing with jingling bells.

79

Sleep! My baby, sleep!
The parrots and the birds rest,
Only my royal prince is not resting. [109]

A baby comes out of the cradle, crawls for a while and then starts taking small steps, holding his mother's hand as adults utter, *"pa, pa, pagali"*. [110]

The Child's First Steps

The child is born in the midst of night,
O little babe, step slowly,
Holding your mother's hand tight. [111]

When children begin to speak, there are songs to help them learn words and speech. These songs, as you will note, are very simple but full of fun and need not always make any sense.

Each line is short, consisting of two or three words. These songs have simple rhyme and rhythm patterns, which are easy for children to remember. Normally, food, birds, trees, flowers, dogs, cats, thieves, queens and kings are the motifs of these rhymes.

A Thief, A Thief, A Thief

I sprinkle curds
I sprinkle milk
I sprinkle water
On my mango tree.
Woman, O woman
Open the door
Who are you? I am a thief
A thief, thief, thief.

Why have you come?
The royal queen
Fell from the palace
She broke her head
So she wanted

A ripe watermelon.
A melon, melon, melon. [112]

The Moon Cake

The moon-cake[113]
Ghee[114] you take
Dip the cake
Into the *ghee*
All children
Eat the half
My dear child
Gets the full
Happa. [115]

When children get a little older, they love to play in groups. They sit or stand in a circle and, clapping their hands, sing nursery rhymes. In some songs, one asks a question and the group answers. These rhymes satisfy their play instinct to climb, jump, run, chase, hide and count.

Play songs

Brother, brother,
Where are your hands?

Group: In the dung.
What did you get from the dung?

Group: A rupee.
What did you do with the rupee?

Group: Gave it to the potter.
What did the potter give?

| Group: | He gave me a pot. |
| | What did you do with the pot? |

| Group: | Dipped it in the well. |
| | What did the well give? |

| Group: | The well gave me water. |
| | What did you do with the water? |

| Group: | Sprinkled it in the garden. |
| | What did the garden give? |

| **Group:** | The garden gave me a flower. |
| | What did you do with the flower? |

| Group: | Offered it to Lord Shiva. |
| | What did Lord Shiva give? |

| Group: | Shiva gave me a sweet ball. |
| | What did you do with the sweetball? |

| Group: | Half did I eat and the other half — |
| | a dog snatched and ran away![116] |

In the above song, children sit in a circle with both their palms touching the ground and repeat the rhyme. One child stands in the centre asking questions. As soon as they say, "A dog snatched and ran away," they all stand up and run off in different directions, acting as dogs. The child in the centre tries to catch one of them; the one caught comes to the centre of the circle, and the children repeat the game.

Love songs

Love songs often express deep emotions between men and women. They can convey messages about being attracted to one another, loneliness, pain and ecstasy.

82

Kum-Kum Mark

Who is that girl with a mark of kum-kum on her forehead ?
Her mark is glittering
And I am bewitched by her!

Who is that girl with coiled hair ?
Her hair is glistering
And I am bewitched by her!

Who is that girl with bangles on her arms?
Her bangles are glistering
And I am bewitched by her![117]

The song above expresses a young man's attraction to, and admiration for, his lover. Even what she wears captivates him. The song below expresses the man's desire for his lover to the point that he wants to devour her.

Let Me Chew Her

My sweetheart is like a betel leaf,
Let me chew her up.
My sweetheart is like a clove,
Let me put her in the betel leaf.
My sweetheart is like a nut,
Let me put her in my mouth. [118]

Hearts Stolen

Down to a pond in a flowery garden,
With a golden pitcher on her head
Wearing a silvery *saree*
A young maid goes to fetch water.
There on horseback goes a young lad,
Their eyes meet,
He likes her pitcher, she likes his horse;
Their minds are lost,
Their hearts are stolen. [119]

83

The song above describes love at first sight between a man and a woman. The pond where girls go to fetch water is often the context for such songs. The song below is a *mando*, a Konkani love folksong.

Mando - I

Twelve long years[120]
I have grown up in the house.
Have no fear, mother,
That you have found me no man.

That I play on the guitar
Is known to all in the village.
An angel from heaven will come
And lead me away by the hand.
When he leads me away by the hand,
Come not in my way, mother,
If it is my luck.
I may sit at the bay-window.

The above folksong is sung by Goans. The *mando* is sung in two voices to the accompaniment of the violin, guitar and drum, called *gumott*. The drama of idyllic love in the *mando* is normally made up of four acts. The first act, reveals the maid in-waiting, yearning and hoping for the miracle of love. Hope has its reward, and in the second act, the lover falls into an attitude of adoration.

II

Like the sun and the moon, you shine,
O angel of my love,
So perfect in your beauty, beloved,
That I fall at your feet in worship.

Come to me, angel of my heart,
Touch me but once with your lips.

Your eyes are *mogra* buds,
They shine like a pair of pearls
And dazzle mine eyes.
They hold my heart in thrall.

Quick is the response — and ecstatic the surrender. That is the theme of
the third act of the *mando*.

III

By the wave of the sea
By the light of the moon
By the braid of my hair
I pledge you eternal love.

Come to me, love, look at me, dear
This fragrance of jasmine and *mogras*.[121]

And in the last and final act of this drama love is fulfilled through marriage.
Following is the fourth act.

IV

Our hearts abound with joy.
This home is aglow with light.
Let us pray to God this day.
For the gift of perennial bliss.

May God ever preserve
This fragrance of jasmine and *mogras*.[122]

The Soft Veil

The soft veil slides from her face,
Miss not a moment
Miss not a chance.
Youth glides in a moment,
Miss not a chance.

The bud blossoms into a rose,
The fragrance flies in a moment,
Miss not a moment,
Miss not a chance.
The earthen pitcher is full of water,
The water streams out in a moment,
Miss not a moment,
Miss not a chance. [123]

The song above emphasises the importance of making the best of youth, which is sure to glide away. The message in the song, therefore, is not to miss a moment or chance of investing in love.

I Do not Love Thee

You have not brought me bangles,
O my sweetheart, I do not love thee.

You have not brought me a *saree*,
O my sweetheart, I do not love thee.

You have not brought me a necklace,
O my sweetheart, I do not love thee. [124]

The Gujerati song above voices the expectations a wife or a woman has of her lover. Since he has not bought any ornaments with which to adorn herself, she is complaining to the point of rejecting him.

A Broken Bowl

A Jogi is standing on the bank of the pond,
He has put on a silken garment
And an orange turban on his head.
I love the Jogi; he has stolen my heart.

O Prembai! You dine from a golden dish.
How will you like his broken bowl?

No, Bhabhi, I love his broken bowl.
His broken bowl has stolen my heart.

O Prembai! You live in a fine palace.
How will you like his broken hut?
No, Bhabhi, I love his broken hut.
His broken hut has stolen my heart.

O Prembai! You sleep on a soft bed.
How will you like his torn carpet?
No, Bhabhi, I love his torn carpet.
His torn carpet has stolen my heart. [125]

This is a playful song by a young girl, named Prembai who is in love. She shares the song with her sister-in-law (or brother's wife). Girls often reveal their secret feelings of love for a man to their sisters-in-law. In the song, the sister-in-law is testing Prembai's love for Jogi, the man she loves.

Marriage songs

Marriage ceremonies are often filled with festive songs. These festivities can go on for several days, according to the ritual requirements of a community. Selecting a bride, buying clothes and ornaments, erecting a *pandal* or a stage where the ceremony is to take place, and organising invitations, dinner, and the bridal send-off ceremony are all done with songs. Girls get glimpses of married life through songs. In their new life, they will have to face mothers-in-law, fathers-in-law and sisters-in-law. Life's lessons are taught indirectly through simple songs.

Bride's Song

(1)
Mother, O mother, I do not want your *saree* of silk.
I am ever grateful for my birth
And a few drops of thy milk.

(2)
In my courtyard is a *mogra* plant.
Bhabbi is a great thief.
She has stolen my brother's heart;
He forgets all his work.

(3)
My Bhabbi is a great thief.
She has stolen my brother's heart;
He forgets all his work.

(4)
The sky gave me my birth,
The earth held me up,
My mother brought me up,
My father gave me in marriage,
The carriage of my husband was ready,
Steady was my brother in sending me off.

(5)
My father reared me with all affection.
He gave me all protection,
Just to give me away to a strange home.

(6)
My father gave his daughter away to a far land.
Never did he care to know again,
Whether I lived or died.

(7)
In the temple of the goddess, entering I pray.
On leaving I ask her to protect,
My eyes, forehead-mark and my braided hair.

(8)
In the temple of the goddess, entering I worship,

On leaving, I ask her to guard
My bracelets forever.

(9)
At the pond, meet a daughter and her mother.
Embracing they wept there,
Filling the pond with their tears. [126]

Morning Song

A parrot sings early in the morning
Perching on a high platform.
Hearing the song of the parrot
Lord Shiva, the husband of Parvati awoke
And began to plan for the marriage of the bride.
From the bed, Dhanjibhai awoke.
He is the husband of Kankuben,
He also began to plan the marriage,
The marriage of his daughter. [127]

The song above emphasises the importance of parents arranging marriages for their children, especially daughters. The marriage arrangements may include selecting the right suitor, providing dowry, and planning the wedding.

In the marriage ceremony, the bridegroom is adorned with beautiful clothes, ornaments and flowers. Traditionally, he is expected to ride a horse and his relatives and friends go in a highly decorated procession, singing and dancing.

Bhari rey bhari nagari

Bhari rey bhari nagari, bhariyeli gajey rey.
Nanubhai na kuverba to gajara-o magey rey
Dhiran rey dhiran kuverba, dhiran dhiran bolo rey,
Pahelun vahana avey teney vahi java diyo rey;
Biju vahana avey teney vahi java diyo rey;

89

Bijun vahana avey tema gajara o avey rey;
Bhari rey bhari nagari, bhariyeli gajey rey.
Nanubhai na kuverba to kanku-o magey rey.
Dhiran rey dhiran kuverba, dhiran dhiran bolo rey,
Pahelun vahana avey teney vahi java diyo rey;
Bijun vahana avey tema kanku-o avey rey.

The Village Is Resounding

The village is resounding with the music of the band
The bride-daughter of Nanubhai asks for the garlands.

Speak softly, O bride, let the first ship sail away,
In the second one comes the garlands of flowers.

The village is resounding with the music of the band,
The bride asks for kum-kum, the red powder.

Speak slowly, O bride, let the first ship sail away,
In the second one come the bags of kum-kum. [128]

Fatana

Fatana are songs of humour and fun. They are sung during a marriage ceremony to reduce the tension under which the girl's side of the family finds itself. There is anxiety on the part of the parents because they have to give away their daughter in marriage and, depending on the custom of their particular community, dowry and entertainment for the wedding may also have to be arranged.

The subjects of these songs are the bride, bridegroom and the in-laws. These songs are sung to tease the participants and to make them laugh. Though the jokes used in these songs are sometimes coarse, no offence is normally taken.

A Tortoise

Here comes a marriage procession of a tortoise.
I won't marry the tortoise,

He hides his face, he hides his hands,
I won't marry the tortoise. [129]

The song is sung to belittle the bridegroom, while the two songs below
are meant to poke fun at the bridegroom's father and the bride's mother.

A Male Cat

Below the seat of the groom is a male cat.
He says *miaou, miaou*;
The cat says: Give me a handful of food, daughter;
Or I will remain here as the bridegroom's father. [130]

A Female Cat

Below the seat of the bride is a female cat,
She says: *miaou, miaou*;
She says: Give me a handful of sweets, son;
Or I will remain here as the bride's mother. [131]

In the marriage ceremony, the most touching scene is probably the *Kanya-Vidaya*, sending off the bride to her new home. All her friends and relatives,
young and old, gather to bid her farerwell and give her their blessings.

Farewell Song

Sita, the bride, is weeping so bitterly,
She has filled the pond with her tears.

Who is going to bid farewell to our bride, Sita?
Her father is going to bid her farewell;
Her mother is going to bid her farewell;
Her brother is going to bid her farewell;
Leaving her home, she is weeping bitterly.

Our Sitabai is going to her husband's home.
Singing a song of farewell, we bless you.
Remember the words of advice from your elders.

91

You lead a holy life and follow the steps of *Tulsi*[132]
Love your new home and preserve its credit,
Listen to what your mother-in-law says,
Be obedient to your father-in-law. [133]

My Daughter is Gone

Early in the morning the mother sweeps the threshold,
Sweeping she searches for the foot-marks of her daughter.

O, my daughter! In vain do I search for your footprints,
How can they remain in the dust so long?

They are not there, my sweet daughter,
They are all rubbed off, my daughter. [134]

Once the bride leaves her home, she has to face a different and sometimes difficult world living with in-laws. Traditionally, the new wife stays with her husband's family. There are songs to reflect the demands of the in-laws on the new bride and her struggle to find her place in the new household and seek independence.

My Husband's Home

In my husband's home, my mother-in-law is a serpent.
Sneering, she asks me to grind the mill all day long.

In my husband's home, my sister-in-law is a dragon;
Snarling, she asks me to spin the *charkha*[135] all night.

In my husband's home, my other sister-in-law is an angel of death;
Scolding me, she eats away my soul all day and night. [136]

A Teak Tree

A teak tree has grown in my yard,
On it sits a cunning crow.

It crows in the first part of the night.
My mother-in-law since then harasses me
And asks me to get up and grind the mill.

O my husband, cut the teak tree
So that the crow will not sit upon it,
The crow will not sit and will not caw,
And my mother-in-law will not harass me.
In peace, I'll sleep the whole night.
O my husband, cut the teak tree.

And from the teak tree make me a pounding pole.
Call the carpenter from Surat to cut;
Call the iron smith to forge the ring;
Call the painter from Baroda to paint,

And let me have the pretty pounding pole.
I will pound the rice till I sweat and grow tired.
O my husband, cut the teak tree and let the crow fly. [137]

The domestic struggle between the bride and the in-laws is not always one-sided. While the bride may express her frustrations in her new home, the in-laws may have their own concerns about the new bride asserting herself.

New Bride

The new bride has come to the house.
She says she is the owner of the house.
She says: This belongs to me and that to you.

The new bride has come to the house.
She came quarrelling with her mother-in-law;
She came harassing her father-in-law;
She came scolding her sister-in-law.
The new bride has come to the house.
She came asking for a separate kitchen. [138]

Work songs

There is a genre of songs sung while working. Work, especially physical labour, ceases to be boring when it is accompanied by song and music. It becomes a rhythmic outlet instead of a monotonous drudgery. At home, as in the fields, there is always plenty of work to do. Women, for example, prefer to work in groups and sing as they perform their chores. This work may include cooking, rolling *chapatis* or *papads*, washing clothes, grinding corn, pounding rice, sowing seeds, or weeding the fields.

Morning Music

Grinding the corn is going on in every house,
It sounds like a flute,
Awake, my husband, it is morning.

Churning is going on in every house;
It sounds like musical instruments,
Awake, my husband, it is morning.

Cleaning vessels is going on in every house;
It sounds like cymbals,
Awake, my husband, it is morning.

Sprinkling of water is going on in every house;
It sounds like showers of rain,
Awake, my husband, it is morning.

Sweeping is going on in every house;
It sounds like wind sweeping the world,
Awake, my husband, it is morning. [139]

The next song is a wife's complaint about weeding in the scorching sun and a demand that her husband get her items from various cities to protect her.

Weeding

Bhuria, thorns pierce my feet,
Get me a pair of shoes from Bombay;
I hate to weed in the scorching sun.

94

Bhuria, I burn in the scorching heat of the sun,
Get me an umbrella from the city of Surat;
I hate to weed in the scorching sun.

Bhuria, toiling in the field, my throat becomes dry,
Get me the best bowl from Broach;
I hate to weed in the scorching sun. [140]

The following song is about the pleasure of reaping — after working in the fields.

Gasigyn Katava Gayeti Zaveri

Gasiyun Katava gayeeti zaveri,
Gasiyun katava gayeeti rey lol,
Mathey chhey ghasa ni puli zaveri,
Hathey chhey pana na bidan rey lol,
Ubhi bazaarey gayee ti zaveri,
Ubhi bazaarey gayeeti ti rey lol,
Ponchi per mana mohyan zaveri,
Ponchi per mohya rey lol.
Ghughari chhum-chhum boley zaveri,
Ghughari chhum-chhum boley rey lol.

I Went to the Pasture to Cut Grass

I went to the pasture to cut grass,
I got my wages,
I went to the bazaar,
A sheaf on my head.
I went to the goldsmith
I saw the wristlet,
I bought the anklet.
Room zoom, room zoom
Ring the anklet-bells. [141]

Songs of separation

The *viraha-geet* or songs of separation are particularly relevant for East African Asians. As discussed in the introductory chapter, the travel and migration of Indians to East Africa led to long periods of separation between families. The women normally remained back in India while the men travelled and made new homes in East Africa. Often, a wife did not know when her husband would return or whether he would return at all. Many times, she found expression for her longings and fears in songs.

How Will You Do Without Me in Foreign Lands?

Don't you remember, O my sweet husband?
We were sitting together on a single swing,
And turn by turn, were swinging with a silken string;
How will you do without me in foreign lands?

Don't you remember, O my sweet husband?
We were dining together from the same dish;
And were talking about our joys and sorrows;
How will you do without me in foreign lands?

My sweet husband, if you had to go away,
Why did you call me and then reject me?
I fail, I faint, I burn within,
How will you do without me in foreign lands?[142]

Sad and Pale

After a lapse of twelve long years
Your beloved has come home,
And you seem so sad and pale, my love.

I sailed the seas for twelve long years,
And brought precious ornaments for you;
Yet you seem so sad and pale, my love.[143]

Kagaliyan

Avati ne jati vhala vadiyama raheti vhala,
Kuva ney todey vata joti, Shamaliya vhala.

Bara bara varasey rey taran aivan kagaliyan vhala,
Kagal na vanchanara nahi rey, Shamaliya vhala.

Sankadi sheri ma maila mehtaji vhala,
Kagaliyan vanchta javo rey, Shamaliya vhala.

Gama ney padarey vadalo ropavo beni,
Vadala ney chhayen kagal vanchun, Shamaliya vhala.

Vadala ney shoban to chotaro bandhavo beni
Chotarey besi ney kagal vanchu, Shamaliya vhala.

Chotara ney shobanti khursi melavo beni
Khursi besi ney kagal vanchu, Shamaliya vhala.

Khursi ney shobanta divada melavo beni,
Divada ajavaley kagal vanchun Shamaliya vhala.

Sasu nu boilun ney Sasara nu boilun vhala,
Marun to nam na hoy rey Shamaliya vhala.

Sasu no jayo ney Sasarano beto vhala,
Maro to kain na sago rey Shamaliya vhala.

A Letter

O my dear husband, you have gone far,
Far in the south countries.

Here in the banyan grove
While fetching water from the well.

97

Every day for twelve years, standing on the well-step,
I have eagerly waited, longing for your letter.
And truly after twelve years the letter came.

But there was none in the whole village to read it to me.

Meantime a school-master met me in a narrow lane,
To read it I requested so joyfully.

Grow a banyan tree at the village square, he said;
I shall read your letter under its cool shade.

Get a platform built under the banyan tree,
Then I shall read your letter sitting on it.

Place on it a chair worthy of the platform,
Then shall I read your letter sitting on it.

Light lamps round about the chairs,
In that light only shall I read your letter.

He read the names of my mother-in-law and father-in-law;
But there was no mention whatsoever of my name![144]

Alas! My husband! You are not my husband!
You are only the son of your father and mother!

A Fair

A fair is held in the city of Surat,
All kinds of *sarees*[145] are sold here;
But my beloved one is not at home.
He is sailing on the deep seas.
If my beloved were here, he would buy all for me,

O, these strangers are buying them up.
My husband is not at home today,
He is sailing on the deep seas.

Months

In the month of *Kartika*,
Kanji, my husband, went to the lands afar,
Leaving me all alone at home.

In the month of *Magsher*
Kanji, my husband, settled there,
Leaving the trees lamenting here.

In the month of *Posha*
Is the month of our love.
Why have you gone discarding that love?

In the month of *Masha*
The bed has become my enemy.
Sleepless do I pass the whole night.

The month of Fagan blossomed —
Blossomed into flowers of *Kesuda*[146]
The gardener brings the flowers of *Mogra*

In the month of *Chaitra*
The *Champaka* was planted.
I gathered its flowers for my beloved.

In the month of *Vaishakha*
The mangoes were picked from the tree.
I prepared its juice for my beloved.

The month of *Jetha* passed away,
And my beloved did not appear;
With whom shall I drink the juice?

The dark month of *Ashadha*
Poured down in showers soft.
The lightning flashed in the sky.

The month of *Shravana*
Torrents filled the pond, rivers overflowing;
How shall my dear one cross them?

The month of *Bhadarva*
Thundered with rage,
Thunder in the soil, seas and sky.

In the month of *Aswin*, too,
O beloved! You did not come.
Diwali decor is fading, waiting do I fade. [147]

Come Home

My sweetheart, why did you go abroad?
Don't you forget to write a piece of paper;
The pangs of separation wring my heart.

My sweetheart, please come home for the four months of monsoon,
Lest you catch cold in this wet season.
When I go to the gardens
I feel so happy; but coming home I burn to ashes.

My sweetheart, please come home for the four months of winter,
Lest you shiver in that cold season.
As the birds eat up seed corn unless it is guarded,
How can I be safe without my master?

My sweetheart, come home for the four months of summer,
Lest you burn in that hot season;
The creepers are dying without water,
From their roots emerge burning fire. [148]

Songs of the sea

The songs of the sea as mentioned in Chapter One are known as *abavani* songs, literally, the language of the sea. In the monsoon season, when the fishermen and sailors travel, they sing *abavani* songs when they load and unload the ship. It is likely that such songs were sung when ships travelled from Bombay or other Indian ports to the East African coast. The rhythm of the songs gives the sailors timing to row and pull the ropes to adjust the sails.

Every small movement has its musical rhythm. The drudgery and monotony of work is lessened when accompanied by rhythmic songs. Songs may be sung while washing the sails or measuring the depth of the sea-water with a rope. These songs are sung for days and nights on end. While lifting heavy timber and other loads, the *kaviyo*, the leader of the group, sings the song in such a way that by repeating a word or rhythmic phrase the strength required for different types of work is regulated and controlled. For example, for quick work with a fast tempo, the leader sings the following while the group then responds with, *"Hayee samal hobelan"*

> O young men, pull
> O young men, pull as you can
> *Hayee samal hobelan.*
>
> Hands at length, use your strength
> *Hayee samal hobelan.*
>
> O the group, all the troop
> *Hayee samal hobelan*[149].

Songs are also composed spontaneously with a beat reflecting the tempo of the work. The refrains are sung in the interval, short or long as required.

Dance songs

The most popular and typical folksongs performed among some of the Hindu communities from Gujerat settled in East Africa are those accompanying the *Garba* and *Rasa* dances during the nine-day festival of Navaratri.

The *Garba* dance is performed by womenfolk either in homes, social halls or temples. Songs that accompany *Garba* dances are dedicated to the goddess Amba, also known as *Bhavani Durga* or *Mahakali*. The festival is celebrated for the worship of *Shakti* — the goddess of divine power and strength. Lamps are lit in the temples of these goddesses and are kept burning day and night for nine days.

Where people gather to perform *Garba,* an earthen pot with holes around it and a lamp burning in it is placed in the centre. This pot is called *Garba.* The original word *Garba-dwip* means the lamp in the centre. Women go round this lamp in a circle, clapping their hands to the rhythm of the songs.

Garba songs describe the goddesses, their forms and their powers to invoke blessings and protection; for example, *Garba* songs could describe the twelve months of the year or the separation of Radha from her beloved husband Krishna. Sometimes themes from domestic and married life are also included.

The *Garba* dance is performed by women on other occasions such as during funfairs and marriages. The women, mainly in yellow and red costumes, dance in a rhythmic circular motion, weaving numerous patterns, all clapping together and symbolising a lotus flower with its petals opening and closing. The drum, *dhol*, gives the *'hinch tal'* or the beat, and the flute plays the tune of the song.

Mother Kali

O Mother Kali, you are the queen of the mountain Pavaghdha.
To climb upon your mountain is a real task.
In the valley is lying the city of Champaner with fourteen bazaars.
There they played *Garba* when the goddess came there.
The king held the skirt of her *saree* and she was pleased.
O King, I am pleased with you, ask any boon you like.
You may ask for the welfare of your family and children;
You may ask for elephants and horses if you so please;
You can ask for the throne of the entire Gujerat;
You may ask for the whole world; ask for the sun or the moon;
Such is the power of the goddess Kalika, no poet can describe her greatness. [150]

The next *Garba* song describes a wife's effort to bring her husband home by citing to him all kinds of reasons. In each case, the husband has an appropriate reply and the only time she succeeds is when her husband is told that his wife is dying.

Mendi toe vavi malave
Mendi toe vavi Malavey ne eno ranga gayo Gujerat rey
Mendi ranga lagyo
Diyarey rangi chati angali ney bhahbhi ye rangiya danta.
Aye danta rangi ney bhabhi koney dekhado
Maro viro gayo paradesha rey — Mendi

Tara vira ney jai etalun kahejey key
Taro viro paraney ney gherey avo, — Mendi
Viro paraney toe bhaley paraney
Eni jana kadhajo zakamala rey, — Mendi

Vira tara ney jai etalun kahejey key
Tari madi marey ney gherey avo, — Mendi
Madi marey toe bhaley marey
Eney daatajo vadala heth rey, — Mendi

Tara vira ney jai etalun kahejey key
Tari gori marey ney gherey avo, — Mendi
Tyanthi ghodi virey khedavi ney
Avi ubhi tey zampa bahar rey, — Mendi

Padarey tambu taniyan ney kain
Bhabhi na bola sambhbalay rey. — Mendi
Ahey sahyabani gori hasey eney
Chhetari bolaviyo ghere rey. — Mendi
Padarey tambu taniyan ney kain
Bhabhi na bola sambhalay rey, — Mendi

The Myrtle Plant

The myrtle plant is planted in Malava,
Its rich colour reached Gujerat.
Sister-in-law has applied henna,
Brother-in-law coloured his last finger.

103

Sister-in-law coloured her teeth.
Whom do you show your coloured teeth,
When my brother has gone to a foreign land?

Tell my lord that his brother is marrying,
Please come home speedily.
If my brother is marrying,
Let his marriage procession be majestic.

Tell my married one that his mother is dying,
Please come home immediately.
If my mother is dying,
Let her be buried under the banyan tree.

Tell my married one that his true love is dying.
Please come home speedily.
The husband took a speedy horse,
And came to the village pond.

He erected a tent by the pond,
And his wife's voice was heard saying,
When you were quite young, you left me alone,
And you went away to foreign lands, cheating me.
Now that I have deceived you,
You have come home so speedily.[151]

Bells Jingle

Golden is my courtyard,
Silvery is the night;
The night is twinkling,
Hands are clapping in time,
Dancing the ankle-bells jingle.[152]

Permission

No light is better than the moonlight,
Can I go, O mother-in-law

To enjoy *Garba* in such moonlight?
I can't say, my dear daughter-in-law.
You can go if your father-in-law allows.

Can I go, my father-in-law
To enjoy *Garba* dance tonight?
How can I allow you my daughter-in-law?
Ask your brother-in-law.

Can I go, O my brother-in-law
To play *Garba* dance tonight?

I cannot allow you my dear *Bhabbi*,[153]
You better ask your sister-in-law.
May I go, my dear sister-in-law
To take part in *Garba* dance?

How can I permit you my dear *Bhabhi*?
Ask your husband if he allows; then only
You can go to enjoy the *Garba* dance.

O my dear husband,
All have gone —
The farmer's wife,
The tailor's wife,
The porter's wife,
The cobbler's wife,
The carpenter's wife.

All have gone to the *Garba* dance,
May I go to take part in the dance?
You can go to enjoy the *Garba* dance![154]

The following two *Garba* songs depict the life of Krishna, and his playful and teasing attitude towards the *Gopis* — the shepherd women of Gokul. Krishna's separation from his beloved wife, Radha, is also a common theme for *garba* songs.

O, the son of Nanda, you have frustrated me.
You have gone away to Mathura,
Leaving me all alone and deserted.

You said that I was as dear as your soul;
You have gone away to Mathura
Leaving me all alone and deserted.[155]
Behave yourself.
I am going with a pot on my head;
The pot is full of coloured water;
I am a maid of Gokul.

Krishna aims at me,
It comes and strikes my body,
Strikes like an arrow. O Krishna, behave yourself;
Somebody will see to it.
O Krishna, keep yourself away from me;
Please do not hold the end of my *saree*;
It will tear and my mother-in-law,
Shall scold and drive me out of the house.[156]

Songs of death

There are certain songs sung especially at the time of death. While the body is carried by men, women sing dirges called *Ṛayali* in Gujerati; and the men sing *Bhajans* (religious hymns with the *tala* or beat of cymbals) and *pakhavaj[157]* or drum. While the body is burning, the people attending the funeral, sing devotional songs addressing the departing soul.

The Final Call

After a long prayer to God,
The final call has come from Hari.
Here is the invitation from Rama,
Why do you wait now?

On the way to Heaven
There are rivers;
How will you cross them?
My son will give cows to Brahmins;
Holding the tail of the cow
I shall cross the river.

On the way to Heaven
There are plenty of thorns;
How will you walk on them?

My daughter will sweep the lanes
And I shall walk safely. [158]
Yamaraj
O Yamaraj, you are my worthy guest,
I am dwelling in my hut,
To what region are you carrying me away?
I am deeply frightened to see your face.

O Yamaraj, tell me to what region are you carrying me away?[159]

Protect Thy Soul

Protect thy soul from evils
Sing *bhajans* to remember Him;
Or thy soul will not be rescued.

The cart loaded with fuel follows him,
The fuel to serve him as his pyre;
In the earthen vessel is carried the fire,
To set his body on fire. [160]

Life is False

Do not be proud of thy mortal body
Which is composed of five elements.

The body is brittle like an earthen pot.
O the mind-bird, do not be captured
In this cage of life,
For life is illusion,
Life is false.

Thy relatives will weep for a day,
Your mother shall shed tears for her whole life;
Your wife will weep for thirteen days only,
    And will weep in the corner of the house.
    Life is illusion; life is false.

    Your parents will come with you up to the gate,
    Your wife will accompany you to the village outskirts;
    Your friends will carry your bier
    And your own brothers will set fire to your pyre,
    Life is illusion, life is false. [161]

    The following song describes in a glorious way the last ceremony for
a human on earth.

Sonala Keri Chita
Sonala keri chita,
Rupala keri kaya,
Sonala keri jwala jale,
Rupala dhurnado jai akas.

A Golden Pyre
A golden pyre,
Silver body,
A golden flame is burning,
Silver smoke is rising to the sky. [162]

Review questions

1. Select a song from each of the above sections in this chapter and discuss
    its meaning.

2. Write and discuss a song you know that falls under any of the categories mentioned in this chapter.
3. Write down five different songs in your language and translate them into English. Determine in what categories they may be classified. Discuss the context in which these songs are used and what message each song conveys?

Project suggestions

1. Organise a class session on songs from your respective communities. Focus on a specific theme. Share and discuss the songs.
2. Invite a group of singers from a selected community. Have them recite some songs. Learn and discuss the meanings of the songs.

NOTES

1   Referred to people who migrated from the Indian sub-continent, currently comprising of India, Pakistan and Bangladesh. Historically, Indians in East Africa have been referred to as Asians. The term "Asian" and "Indian" is used interchangeably in this book.

2   R. Walji, Shirin, *A History of the Ismaili Community in Tanzania,* p.23.

3   Ibid. p. 23.

4   Ibid. p. 23.

5   J.H. Patterson, *The Man-eaters of Tsavo*, pp. 20-21.

6   C. Salvadori, *We Came in Dhows,* "Why trains slow down at Mackinnon Road." Contributed by Ikram Hassan.Volume I, p. 168.

7   M.G.,Visram, *Red Soils of Tsavo*, p. 104.

8   R. Walji, Shirin, *A History of the Ismaili Community in Tanzania*, p. 23.

9   C. Salvadori, *We Came in Dhows.* "Adrift on a Dhow." Contributed by Abdul Rehman Kana. Vol. I, p. 8.

10   Turning the head right and then left and declaring peace and blessings of God is part of the Muslim prayer ritual.

11   Ibid. "The Worst Dhow Season," Contributed by Karsonbhai Premji Ganji Bhudia. Vol. I, p. 10-11.

12   Ibid. "In Memoriam," Vol. I, p.13. (Composed in 1944. Marciel)

13   M. Patel, *Folksongs of South Gujerat*, p. 4.

14   Ibid. p. 42.

15   Ibid. p. 45.

16   C. Salvadori (1996), *We Came in Dhows.* "An Autobigraphy by Harry Thuku (passim)." Vol. III, p.148.

17   Z. Patel, *Challenge to Colonialism: The Struggle of Alibhai Mulla Jeevanjee for Equal Rights in Kenya*, p. 31.

18   C. Salvadori, *We Came in Dhows,* "An Inspiration, " Contributed by Zarina Patel. Vol. III. p. 188.

19   *Daily Nation.* No. 1367. Thursday, February 25.

20   Translated by Zarina Patel.

21 Naomi Kipury, *Oral Literature of the Maasai*, p. 14.

22 S.K. Akivaga and A.B. Odaga, *Oral Literature: A School Certificate Course*, p. 20.

23 J.B. Noss, *Man's religlions*, 6th Ed., pp. 76-77.

24 Narrated to the authors by Nimaben Shah.

25 G. Reed, *The Talkative Beasts: Myths Fables and Poems of India*, p. 79.

26 Narrated to the authors by Manjula Vaghela. Details cross-referenced with M. Jaffrey, *Seasons of Splendour: Tales, Myths and Legends of India*, p.121.

27 Narrated to the authors by Nimaben Shah. Details cross-referenced with G. Reed, *The Talkative Beasts: Myths Fables and Poems of India*, p. 83.

28 Narrated to the authors by Chandraben Thakker.

29 S.K. Akivaga and A.B. Odaga, *Oral Literature: A School Certificate Course*, p. 30.

30 Narrated to the authors by Manjula Vaghela. Details cross-referenced with M. Jaffrey, *Seasons of Splendour: Tales, Myths and Legends of India*, p. 47.

31 Narrated to the authors by Nimaben Shah.

32 Narrated to the authors by Bilkis Hassanali.

33 Narrated to the authors by Razia Jeewaji.

34 Narrated to the authors by Shirinbai Sukhadwalla. Details cross-referenced with G. Reed, *The Talkative Beasts: Myths, Fables and Poems of India*, I. p. 13.

35 Narrated to the authors by Rubabai Kaderbhai. Details cross-referenced with V. Haviland, *Favorite Fairy Tales Told in India*, p. 22.

36 Narrated to the authors by Jenumbai Kirefu. Details cross-referenced with E.C. Babbit, *Jakarta Tales: Animal Stories*, p. 39.

37 Narrated to the authors by Murtaza Hassanali.

38 Narrated to the authors by Asmabai Mohamedali Hassanali.

39 Narrated to the authors by Zubedaben Abbas Karimbhai.

40 Narrated to the authors by Abid Abbas Karimbhai.

41 Narrated to the authors by Jenumbai Kirefu.

42 Narrated to the authors by Z. Jila and Aban Noor.

43 Narrated to the authors by Sakinabai Karimbhai.

44 Narrated to the authors by Sakinabai Podawalla.

45 Ramesh Mudholkar, *175 Stories of Akbar and Birbal*, p.vii,

46 Stories 20, 21 and 22 narrated to the authors by Bilkis Waliji. Details of Story 22 cross-referenced with R. Mudholkar, *175 Stories of Akbar and Birbal*, p. 69.

47 Narrated to the authors by Ruhabhai Kapasi.

48 C. Withers, and S. Benet, *Riddles of Many Lands*, pp. 125-126.

49 Narrated to the authors by P. Mulkhraj. Details cross-referenced with Withers, C and Benet, S *Riddles of Many Lands*, pp. 125-126.

111

50 R. Mudholkar, 175 *Stories of Akbar and Birbal*, p. 75.

51 Ibid. p. 126.

52 Narrated to the authors by Bilkis Waliji. Details cross-referenced with R. Mudholkar, 175 *Stories of Akbar and Birbal*, p. 126.

53 C. Williams and S. Benet, *Riddles of Many Lands*, p.121

54 Ibid. p. 125.

55 Ibid. p. 125.

56 Ibid. p. 125.

57 Ibid. p. 123.

58 Ibid. p. 125.

59 Ibid. p. 121.

60 Ibid. p. 121.

61 Ibid. p. 123.

62 Ibid. p. 122.

63 Ibid. p. 122.

64 Ibid. p. 122.

65 Ibid. p. 122.

66 Ibid. p. 123.

67 Ibid. p. 123.

68 Ibid. p. 125.

69 Ibid. p. 122.

70 Ibid. p. 123.

71 An alternative version is in Ramesh Mudholkar's *175 Stories of Akbar and Birbal*, p. 32.

72 J. Christian, *Behar Proverbs*, p. 8.

73 Champak C. Shah, *Proverbs of India (A Collection of Gujerati, Marathi, Bengali, Behari, Tamil and Telugu Proverbs)*, p. 11.

74 J. Christian, *Behar Proverbs*, p. 65.

75 Champak C. Shah, *Proverbs of India (A Collection of Gujerati, Marathi, Bengali, Behari, Tamil and Telugu Proverbs)*, p. 36.

76 Ibid. p. 23.

77 Ibid. p. 28.

78 Ibid. p. 9.

79 Ibid. p. 8.

80 Ibid. p. 10.

81 Ibid. p. 10.

82 Ibid. p. 10.

83 Ibid. p. 10.

84 Ibid. p. 26.

85 Ibid. p. 26.

86 Ibid. p. 26.

87 Ibid. p. 14.

88 Ibid. p. 25.

89 J. Christian, *Behar Proverbs*, p. 191.

90 Champak C. Shah, *Proverbs of India (A Collection of Gujerati, Marathi, Bengali, Behari, Tamil and Telugu Proverbs)*, p. 43.

91 Ibid. p. 32.

92 Ibid. p. 20.

93 Ibid. p. 38.

94 Ibid. p. 8.

95 Tulsidas is a famous 16th century Indian poet.

96 J. Christian, *Behar Proverbs*, p. 17.

97 Abul Fazl was a highly learned man. He was one of the Nine Gems in Emperor Akbar's court.

98 Champak C. Shah, *Proverbs of India (A Collection of Gujerati, Marathi, Bengali, Behari, Tamil and Telugu Proverbs)*, p. 31.

99 Ibid. p. 6.

100 Ibid. p. 7.

101 Ibid. p.35.

102 Ibid. p. 35.

103 Ibid. p. 36.

104 J. Christian, *Behar Proverbs*, p. 19.

105 Ibid. p. 57.

106 Champak C. Shah, *Proverbs of India (A Collection of Gujerati, Marathi, Bengali, Behari, Tamil and Telugu Proverbs)*, p. 40.

107 Folk-songs in this chapter are cited with the kind permission of Madhubhai Patel, *Folk-songs of South Gujerat*.

108 Madhubhai Patel, *Folksongs of South Gujerat*, p. 18.

109 Ibid. p. 20.

110 Tiny steps.

111 Ibid. p. 22.

112 Ibid. p. 23.

113 Ibid. p. 22.

114 *Ghee* is calcified butter.

115 *Happa* means food.

116 Ibid. pp. 22-23.

117 Ibid. p. 28.

118 Ibid. p. 28.

119 Ibid. pp. 28-29.

120 Song mentioned by J. Suarez. Text of 'Mando I-IV' quoted from Lucio Rodrigues, Armando Menezes, D.N. Shanbag, *Konkani Folksongs of Goa: An Album.*

121 *Mogra* is a white fragrant flower normally used during worship.

122 Lucio Rodrigues, Armando Menezes, Shanbag, D.N. *Konkani Folksongs of Goa: An Album.*

123 Madhubhai Patel, *Folksongs of South Gujerat*, p. 29.

124 Ibid. p. 29.

125 Ibid. p. 31.

126 Ibid. p. 25.

127 Ibid. p. 32.

128 Ibid. p. 33.

129 Ibid. p. 34.

130 Ibid. p. 37.

131 Ibid. p. 37.

132 *Tulsi* is basil. It is used for both spiritual and medicinal purposes.

133 Ibid. p. 36.

134 Ibd. p. 36.

135 A spinning wheel.

136 Ibid. p. 41.

137 Ibid. p. 41.

138 Ibid. p. 34.

139 Ibid. p. 39.

140 Ibid. p. 40.

141 Ibid. p. 40.

142 Ibid. p. 43.

143 Ibid. p. 42.

144 Traditionally, a husband is expected never to utter his wife's name in public.

145 *Saree* is a dress worn by Indian women. It is a long five to six-yard cloth made of light material and wrapped around the waist and over the shoulders.

146 *Kesuda* are orange flowers used during worship.

147 Ibid. p. 45.

148 Ibid. p. 46.

149 Ibid. p. 48.

150 Ibid. p. 51.

151 Ibid. p. 57.

152 Ibid. p. 52.

153 *Bhabbi* means brother's wife.

154 Ibid. p. 52.

155 Ibid. p. 55.

156 Ibid. p. 55.

157 *Pakhvaj* also means perfect sound.

158 Ibid. p. 72.

159 Ibid. p. 73.

160 Ibid. p. 73.

161 Ibid. p. 74.

162 Ibid. p. 74.

BIBLIOGRAPHY

Akivaga, S. K., and A.B. Odaga, *Oral Literature: A School Certificate Course.* Nairobi: East African Educational Publishers, 1982.

Babbit, Ellen C. *Jataka Tales.* New York: Appleton-Century Craft, 1981.

Carroll, Dihari, et al., eds. *Wonders of Man.* New York: Arthur Dembner Publishers, 1972.

Chaudhuri, K.N. *Asia Before Europe: Economy and Civilisation of the Indian Ocean from the Rise of Islam to 1750.* Cambridge University Press, 1990.

Chaudhuri, K.N. *Trade and Civilization in the Indian Ocean: An Economic History from the Rise of Islam to 1750.* Cambridge University Press, 1985.

Christian, J. *Behar Proverbs.* Kegan Paul, Trench, Trubner & Co., Limited, 1691.

Delf, G. *Asians in East Africa.* 1886 to 1945. London: Oxford University Press, 1963.

Emeneau, M.B., and A. Taylor, "Annamese Arabic and Punjabi Riddles." *Journal of America Folklore*, LVII 12-20. 1945.

Ghai, D. ed. *Portrait of the Minority: Asians in East Africa.* Nairobi: Oxford University Press, 1965.

Had, J. *Types of Indic Oral Tales Supplement FF Communication #242.* Snomalainen Tiedeakatemia. Academia Scientiarium Fennical. Helsinki, 1988.

Haviland, Virginia. *Favourite Fairy Tales Told in India.* Boston: Little Brown and Company. 1973.

Hollingsworth, L. W. *Asians of East Africa.* London, 1960.

Jaffrey, Madhur. *Seasons of Splendour: Tales. Myths, and Legends of India.* New York: Atheneum, 1985.

Kipury, Naomi, *Oral Literature of the Maasai.* Nairobi: East African Educational Publishers, 1983.

Mangat, J.S. *A History of the Asians in East Africa.* Oxford, 1969.

Mudholkar, R. *175 Stories of Akbar and Birbal.* Pune 2. India: Anmol Prakashan, n.d.

Munshi, R.N. "A Few Parsee Riddles." *Journal of the Anthropological Society of Bombay.* 1915.

Lucio Rodrigues, Armando Menezes, Shanbag, D.N. *Konkani Folksongs of Goa: An Album.*Department of Sanskrit, Karnatak University. Dharwar.

Noss, J.B. *Man's Religions.* 6th Edition New York: Macmillan Publishers Co., Inc., 1980.

Ogot, B. A. and J.K. Kieran, eds. *Zamani: A Survey of East African History.* Nairobi: East African Publishing, 1968.

Patterson, J.H. *The Man-eaters of Tsavo.* London: Macmillan Publishers, 1907.

Patel, M. *Folksongs of South Gujerat.* Gackwad Prinatrance Private Ltd., 1974.

Patel, Z. *Challenge to Colonialism.The Struggle of Alibhai Mulla Jeevanjee for Equal Rights in Kenya:* The Standard Limited. 1997.

Pepicello, W J., and A. Green, *The Language of Riddles,* Columbus: Ohio State University Press, 1984.

Reed, Gwandolyn. *The Talking Beasts: Myths. Fables and Poems of India.* New York: Lothrop, Lee and Shepard Co, 1969.

Salvadori, C. *Through Open Doors: A View of Asian Cultures in Kenya.* Nairobi: Kenway Publications, 1983.

Salvadori, C. *We Came in Dhows.* Nairobi: Paperchase Kenya Ltd., 1996.

Shah, Champak C. *Proverbs of India* (A Collection of Gujerati. Marathi, Bengali, Punjabi, Kashmeri, Behari. Tamil and Telugu Proverbs). Jiraid, Kansas: Haldeman-Julius Company, 1923.

Shannon, G. *Stories to Solve: Folktales from Around the World.* New York: Greenwillow Books, 1985.

Taylor, A. *English Riddles from Oral Tradition.* Berkeley University of California Press, 1951

Vansina, J. and J.M. Wright, *Oral Tradition: A Study on the Historical Methodology.* Chicago: 1965.

Vatuk, V.P. *Studies in Indian Folk Traditions.* Manohar Publications, 1979.

Visram M.G. *Red Soils of Tsavo.* Previously published as *(On a Plantation in Kenya.)* p. 104. Mombasa. Kenya, 1987.

Walji, S.R. *History of the Ismaili Community in Tanzania.* Doctoral dissertation. University of Wisconsin, Madison, 1974.

Withers, C., and S. Benet. *5 Riddles of Many Lands.* New York: Abelard-Schuman, 1956.

INDEX